T0311124

The University of Groningen in the World

The University of Groningen in the World

A Concise History

Klaas van Berkel & Guus Termeer

PALLAS PUBLICATIONS

Cover illustration: all the photographs on the cover are also included inside the book on the following pages: 12, 15, 17, 32, 52, 59, 78, 80, 92, 106, 112, 119, 125, 129 & 130
Cover design and lay-out: Margreet van de Burgt

ISBN   978 90 8555 123 2 [paperback]
ISBN   978 90 8555 124 9 [hardback]
e-ISBN 978 90 4855 505 5
DOI   10.5117/9789056297848
NUR   694

© University of Groningen 2021

Contents

Preface

Before you lies a publication that is the fulfilment of a long-cherished dream of the University of Groningen (UG) to have an up-to-date, concise and smoothly written book on the history of this university. It is an interesting read for anyone who is connected with the UG, but it has been written in particular for international students, staff members, visitors and other interested parties.

When getting to know and understand someone, an effective method is to learn about important details from their past. This is also true, mutatis mutandis, with regard to organizations and institutions. How and why has something become what it eventually is? What makes something unique? What are its red flags, idiosyncrasies, achievements and failures? What elicits pride but perhaps also shame? Can an essential core be identified?

The authors Klaas van Berkel and Guus Termeer have succeeded outstandingly in answering these questions. The task could not have been fulfilled better by anyone else. Van Berkel is a renowned Dutch historian and professor. As the author of a three-volume standard work on the history of Groningen's university, he is the expert par excellence on this subject. Termeer, who wrote the sections on the university's twentieth-century history, is uniquely equipped to provide his vision on UG's most recent decades given his involvement as a former editor-in-chief of the university newspaper the *UK* and a coordinator/organizer of *Studium Generale* activities.

I find the most valuable historical works to be those that conjure 'a historical experience' for me. I have always enjoyed absorbing interesting facts and intelligent interpretations – in brief, the story that has been composed. But what I also look for is insight, often in the form of epiphanies, that shows that I've understood something fully. This 'eureka' moment came for me in this book when I realized: Of course, now I understand it! That is why the centre of a beautiful, medium-sized city in the northern Netherlands houses such a venerable, old and classic university that belongs among the top 100 universities worldwide! That is

why so many international students and researchers choose to pursue their academic interests here! That is why there is so much interdisciplinary collaboration and why the university is characterized by such short lines of communication!

I wish you many similar insights but also just as much pleasure as I had reading the text and looking at the beautiful illustrations.

Prof. Jouke de Vries
President of the Board of the University of Groningen

Introduction

History matters. Who and what we are is in part determined by our history. This is also true of universities. The buildings, the degree programmes on offer, and the way a university is administered all bear traces of the past: nothing ever appears in a vacuum, and there is nothing that comes from nothing. Anyone who comes into contact with the University of Groningen and wishes to understand something of its character and purpose is therefore well advised to also explore the university's history. How did the University of Groningen grow from a provincial institution established for religious reasons into a national university with 36,000 students, of whom 25% come from abroad, and an academic staff, of whom 45% come from outside the Netherlands?

The leitmotif in this book is our thesis that the University of Groningen has been an international university not only since the last decades of the 20th century but since its foundation in 1614. The first professors formed a rich international community, and many students came from outside the Republic of the United Netherlands, especially from areas now belonging to Germany. Internationalization, a slogan that has been all the rage in recent decades, is therefore nothing new for the University of Groningen. Its meaning, though, has changed over time. Sometimes it has referred to the proportion of international students among the Groningen student population, sometimes to the international standing of Groningen science, and sometimes to the safe haven that Groningen offered to students and scholars who no longer felt safe in their own countries. Even in the late 19th century, when the national character of the university was most emphasized, when Groningen had almost no international students and nationalism was in its heyday, the international significance of Groningen scholars was perhaps at its peak and internationalism blossomed like never before. History therefore also gives us some food for thought.

Can a journey through the history of the University of Groningen also teach us something about its character and identity? In many ways, the university's history followed that of other Dutch and European universities. Neither its blossoming in the 17th century nor its subsequent decline in the late 18th century is unique to Groningen. And yet, in one respect at least, Groningen history differs from that of other universities in the Netherlands in one important way, namely the university's location in the extreme north of the country, close to the German border and far from the cultural and economic hubs in the west and centre of the country. Its proximity to Germany was an advantage in the 17th century, while its remoteness was often problematic, especially from the 19th century onwards. The fact that Groningen was so far removed from the political and economic centre of the Netherlands – and therefore remained small for a relatively long time – sometimes compelled the university's administrators to take unconventional steps. Groningen could not afford to think only in terms of existing frameworks and was forced at times to take unorthodox measures. It is not a complete coincidence that Groningen was the first Dutch university to appoint a Jewish professor, to welcome a female student or to appoint a female lecturer. It is also interesting to note that once their international reputation was secured, scholars often chose to settle at this relatively small university, where they were less burdened with administrative and teaching cares than at larger universities. Examples include the astronomer Jacobus Kapteyn, the philosopher and psychologist Gerardus Heymans, and the professor of comparative religion Gerardus van der Leeuw. Whether this is sufficient to claim a unique Groningen identity is something we leave to the reader to decide.

Klaas van Berkel
Guus Termeer

1

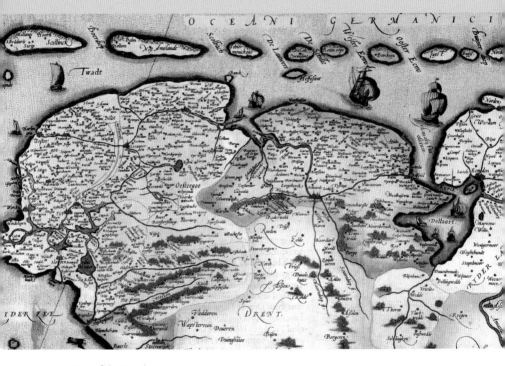

1. Map of the Northern Netherlands and East Frisia, by Abraham Ortelius, 1568.

12

Early heyday (1614-1714)

In the area between the Schelde and Eems rivers, now known as the Netherlands, there were no universities in the Middle Ages. It was only at the time of the revolt of the Dutch provinces against Spanish rule, which began around 1570, that new universities were founded north of the big rivers: first in Leiden (1575), later in Franeker (1585), and then in Groningen in 1614. This was followed by Utrecht (1636) and Harderwijk (1648). It is interesting to note that these universities almost immediately gained international renown for the high quality of their education and the fame of the scholars they attracted. Dutch science and scholarship, both inside and outside university walls, greatly contributed to the Golden Age of the newly formed Republic of the Seven United Netherlands. The University of Groningen played an important role in this context.

What came before

The University of Groningen may boast a long and respectable history, but it is not one of Europe's oldest universities. By the time it was founded in 1614, other countries had already had universities for a few centuries, and the standard model of *the* university had been fully formed. The first universities (Bologna, Paris and Oxford) had all begun in their own way – some as corporations of students who hired teachers, others as corporations of teachers who attracted students. But by the 15th century, it was more or less clear what a university was: an institution of higher education with the right to bestow certain degrees having a civil effect (namely a license to practice law or medicine). This civil effect was guaranteed by a sovereign: the Pope as head of the Catholic Church, the German Emperor, or the sovereign of a specific country. For example, the oldest university of the Low Countries, the University of Leuven, was founded in 1425 thanks to a papal bull issued by Pope Martin V. The highest degree a student could obtain was that of 'doctor', but the degrees of 'master' (magister) and 'licentiate' were also prized.

Students moved from university to university, and teachers were also surprisingly mobile, which was partially facilitated by the fact that classes were taught in Latin everywhere. Together, students and teachers were responsible for the fact that by 1500, a truly European system of higher education was in place.

The provincial noblemen and members of the ruling elite who founded the University of Groningen in 1614 were acutely aware of the need to integrate the new university into this centuries-old European system. But they also knew that the new university was part of an older, more regional scholarly tradition going at least as far back as the late 15th century. Around 1480, in a Cistercian monastery in the nearby village of Aduard, Groningen humanists and theologians had gathered at the abbot's invitation to exchange ideas and teach the monks about new developments in scholarship. This was known as the Aduard Circle, a unique phenomenon at the time in the northern Netherlands and the neighbouring German regions. Visitors to Aduard found a community that more closely resembled an academy than a monastery.

One man who played a central role in the Aduard Circle was the theologian Wessel Gansfort (1419-1489). With his criticism of various practices and dogmas within the Catholic Church and his emphasis on reading the Bible in the original languages, he became known as a precursor of the Protestant Reformation – a split within the Christian Church that led to the creation of independent Protestant churches (Dutch Mennonite, Lutheran and Calvinist). He was one of the

2. Maquette of the St. Bernardus Abbey in Aduard, founded in 1192 and destroyed in the late 16th century. The only building still standing is the rectangular building at the bottom left. It was the infirmary of the abbey but now serves as a Dutch Reformed Church.

3. Stained glass
window in the uni-
versity auditorium,
by Johan Dijkstra
(finished in 1951). This
window represents
the Aduard Circle,
with Wessel Gansfort
standing and Rudolf
Agricola sitting at
the organ.

first in the northern Netherlands to become fluent in Hebrew. Another influential figure was the much younger humanist Rudolf Agricola (1444-1485), who immersed himself in the culture of the Renaissance in Italy, where he also mastered the finesses of Latin. Following his Italian apprenticeship, he worked for some time as secretary and diplomat at the service of the Groningen city authorities. At the time, the city ruled over much of its surroundings (the Ommelanden) and formed a semi-independent city-state. Agricola frequently visited Aduard.

Founding the university

Groningen's independent position came to an end in the 16th century. The city and surrounding area were absorbed, not without a struggle, into the Habsburg Empire under Emperor Charles V (King of Spain and ruler of the Netherlands). Groningen was also greatly impacted by the Reformation. All of this combined to make Aduard's position highly precarious, and the monastery eventually lost its significance as a meeting place for scholars. In the meantime, within the safety of the walled city of Groningen, the theologian and humanist Regnerus Praedinius (1510-1559) helped to make the Latin School – a grammar school preparing the students for university – a great success. A late follower of Gansfort and Agricola and an admirer of Erasmus, Praedinius attracted students from all over Europe, introducing forms of academic education that allowed his students to shorten their expensive stay abroad. The only university in the Netherlands at that time was in faraway Leuven, which was heavily dominated by Catholics, and many of Praedinius' students preferred to attend a Protestant university in Germany (e.g. the Lutheran University of Wittenberg).

The 1560s marked the onset of the Dutch Revolt against the Spanish King Philip II, the son and successor of Charles V. This revolt, born out of discontent over the harsh persecution of Protestants and out of a fear of the loss of city and provincial privileges, was led by William of Orange, who was the Stadtholder of Holland on behalf of the Spanish King. The conflict culminated in the Dutch renouncing Philip II's rule and forming a new state, the Republic of the Seven United Netherlands, in 1581. For a long time, it was unclear which side of the conflict Groningen was on. It was only in 1594 that the city was forced, after a long siege, to join the new Republic. Thereafter, the city and the Ommelanden jointly formed an autonomous province within the Republic. Each province was administered by its own provincial council (States) and a stadtholder, who was the highest civil servant of the provincial council and military commander-in-chief. In Groningen, this position was held by William Louis of Nassau, a nephew of William of Orange. Following Groningen's annexation to the Republic, which included the adoption of the Protestant – and in particular Calvinist (Reformed Protestant) – faith, the Groningen city authorities immediately implemented educational reform. In this context, they recruited Reformed theologian and historian Ubbo Emmius (1547-1625), who was rector of the Latin School in Leer, just across the German border. Emmius' task was to restore the Latin School in Groningen to its former glory – something the East Frisian scholar did with great success.

The young Republic also felt the need for its own Protestant universities. In 1575, the first university of the free north was founded in Leiden, allegedly under

4. *Ubbo Emmius, first rector of the University of Groningen. By an unknown painter, 1618. Emmius was professor of history and geography, which explains the book in his left hand and the small globe on which his right hand rests.*

the auspices of Philip II. After the Netherlands' renunciation of the King of Spain in 1581, the councils of every province claimed sovereignty, thereby gaining the right to establish a university. This led to the establishment of the Republic's second university by the States of Friesland in Franeker in 1585. In the neighbouring province of Groningen, the ruling noblemen and burghers did not yet dare take such a step. Instead, in 1596, they appointed the jurist Mello Brunsema to give lectures in law. This did not qualify as a university since the new law faculty did not have the right to award doctoral degrees (*ius promovendi*). Brunsema's lectures came to an end, and nothing is known about his whereabouts after 1601. But the idea of making higher education possible in Groningen remained, although the ongoing and costly conflict with Spain meant the time was not yet ripe for such an undertaking.

This changed in 1609, when a twelve-year truce was signed with Spain and a fierce conflict erupted between two movements within the dominant Reformed Church: the Remonstrants and the Counter-Remonstrants. The more liberal Remonstrants were strongly represented at the University of Leiden and also seemed to gain a foothold in Franeker, to the objection of the orthodox burgomasters of Groningen and of Ubbo Emmius. This led the States of Groningen (the city and the Ommelanden) to decide in 1612 to establish a university of their own as a bastion of orthodoxy against the Leiden Remonstrants. Following a long and difficult preparation period, the university was finally established in the summer of 1614. A placard was printed, known as the Eternal Edict, announcing the establishment of the new university and containing a eulogy to the city of Groningen. Three messengers were hired to distribute the placard around the Republic, the German Empire and a few cities on the Baltic coast, all the way to distant Danzig.

The University of Groningen officially opened its doors on 23 August 1614. The inaugural ceremony began with a service in the Martinikerk, the city's main church, and continued at the recently renovated former Sywen Convent on Broerstraat, the university's new home. On 23 and 24 August, many speeches were given, a grand banquet was held, and the first rector magnificus was appointed, almost in passing. His name: Ubbo Emmius. To celebrate the official opening, the collected works of Wessel Gansfort were reprinted, thus making it clear that the new institution could claim highly honourable antecedents.

Four faculties

The University of Groningen was a provincial institution, which meant it was financed and controlled by the States of the Province of Groningen, consisting of representatives from the city and its surrounding area. The States appointed a four-member board of curators to oversee the university's activities. Teaching was done by professors, who jointly formed the senate, and from among whose ranks a new rector magnificus was elected every year. The senate drew up nominations for a new professor whenever a vacancy arose, who was then appointed by the States, and it also acted as a court of law for minor offences committed by students (the *forum academicum*). The latter was an important privilege for a university, since it guaranteed that international students who were guilty of an offence (such as reneging on their debts, intimidating women or harassing city guards) were not judged according to harsh and unfamiliar local laws. Instead, they were subjected to the mild judgment of professors, who saw themselves not only as judges but also as educators and were loath to brand youthful delinquents as such for life. Universities were also open to everyone: no special prior education was required.

A university in Europe generally consisted of four faculties: theology, law, medicine, and liberal arts and philosophy. The latter was viewed as a preparatory faculty where students were deemed to start their academic career. Only after being schooled in the basics of logic, rhetoric, classical and oriental languages, mathematics and philosophy were they supposed to progress to one of the three

5. The so-called Eternal Edict, which annouces the foundation of a university at Groningen, 1614. It has been suggested that Ubbo Emmius wrote at least part of this pamphlet.

The Eternal Edict

The placard distributed across Europe in 1614 by the States of Groningen to announce the foundation of the new university described in great detail the exceptional advantages of Groningen as a student city. According to the edict, Groningen was a natural home for the Muses.

> Its charming situation is renowned, the air is clean and wholesome, the food supply abundant and there is a wealth of guesthouses and attendant facilities. For the benefit of this school (...), in past months we have also at great cost furnished lecture halls and buildings, which we keep at the ready in the part of the city most suited for this undertaking, this school of the Muses and academic workplace, away from the bustle and noise of people and their occupations, and near a spacious and exquisite church.

A truly beautiful example of 17th-century marketing!

6. A disputation or dissertation defence in the 17th century. Detail of the title page of Casper Barlaeus, Oratien en blyde inkomst *(Amsterdam 1662). The presiding professor is standing in the pulpit; the defending student is behind the lectern below the pulpit.*

higher faculties. The professors taught lectures but also led exercises in argumentation, known as disputations, in which students defended and opposed a number of theses. Originality and new research were not required: the goal was not to increase knowledge and deepen insight but to train rhetorical skills. Such skills were essential for future ministers and magistrates, and future physicians also needed primarily to be able to present arguments for their diagnosis. At the time, physicians left the actual hands-on work to barber surgeons, who were non-scholars who learned their craft through practice. The final disputation, which allowed a student to officially obtain his doctorate, was called a dissertation and consisted largely of a series of theses that the candidate was asked to defend. Incidentally, students rarely spent their entire studies at a single university. It was far more common to spend some time at various universities before going to a prestigious university abroad to obtain one's doctorate. There was no obligation to follow specific lectures at a university in order to obtain a doctorate there. In this sense too, students at early modern universities were completely free to shape their education to their liking.

Small but international

The University of Groningen remained relatively small for a very long time. In 1614, six professors were appointed at the four faculties, and this number grew only very slowly throughout the 17th century. The first professor to be appointed was Ubbo Emmius, the schoolmaster and historian, who had by that time gained an international reputation with his multi-volume overview of the history of Friesland. Emmius was appointed to teach history and Greek. The second professor was a personal friend of Emmius, Fleming Nicolaus Mulerius, who had previously acted as a city physician in Harlingen and had also been the provincial physician in Friesland and the chief rector of the Latin School in Leeuwarden. Mulerius was tasked with teaching medicine and mathematics and was mostly interested in the latter, in particular astronomy. In 1617, he published a completely revised and newly annotated (third) edition of Nicolaus Copernicus' seminal work, *De revolutionibus orbium coelestium* (*On the Revolutions of the Heavenly Spheres*, originally published in 1543). This work was highly controversial in

7. Nicolaus Mulerius, the first professor of astronomy and medicine. By an unknown painter, 1618. As is shown by the instruments in his hand, he identified himself primarily as an astronomer.

Europe, especially after the warning issued to Galileo by the Catholic Church in 1616, but since Catholic censorship no longer held sway in the Republic, Mulerius was free to publish his edition with the Amsterdam publisher Willem Janszoon Blaeu. Incidentally, conducting research and publishing results were not regular tasks of 17th-century professors, although they were encouraged to acquire a certain degree of fame within the scholarly world.

The other four professors are less well known. Cornelis Pijnacker, previously a professor in Leiden, came to Groningen to teach law, as did Groningen native Johannes Epinus Huninga. A young Scot, William Makdowell, was hired to teach philosophy, while theology was assigned to a young German, Hermann Ravensberger. These six men (there was as yet no place for women at the university)

8. Bird's eye view of the premises of the university in the mid-seventeenth century. Detail of a map of the city of Groningen by Egbert Haubois, 1637. Clearly visible is the Academy Church, with the Academy Building across the street.

formed a nice mix of young talent and experience, but what is most striking is how 'international' a group they were: an East Frisian, a Fleming, a Hollander, someone from Groningen, a Scot and a German. The academic world as a whole was international, in part due to Latin being the language of instruction. It was the language in which lectures were taught and disputations and dissertation defences held, and it was used in official university documents, including the senate's decisions, lecture schedules (also known as *series lectionum*), inaugural lectures by new professors and eulogies upon the death of a professor.

It was not only the professors whose numbers were limited but also the modest facilities at their disposal. The main university building was a former nunnery on Broerstraat. This building (a low complex around a square courtyard entered through a gate on the street side) had room for a few lecture halls, appointed rooms for the senate and curators, and lodgings for the registrar, who was the servant to the rector and responsible for helping him with enrolments but also for keeping the building clean. Across the street was the Broerkerk, where academic ceremonies took place (the opening of the academic year, inaugural lectures, and dissertation defences), with room in the apse for a library and an anatomical theatre. The university library was small and consisted almost entirely of overview and reference works – modern books had to be purchased by the professors themselves (and journals did not yet exist). The anatomical theatre was important, since this was where the professor of medicine conducted his anatomical demonstrations – something Mulerius did only rarely, incidentally. Groningen did not yet possess that other well-known feature of a modern university, a medicinal garden or *hortus botanicus*. It was only in 1642 that steps were taken to create a medicinal garden when an agreement was reached with a local apothecary who kept a garden in the north of the city. It took until the end of the century for a primitive chemistry laboratory to be set up. Student facilities were almost non-existent. From the start, a canteen (*bursa*) was created where students could purchase meals at a small price. There was also a horse trainer (to teach students horse riding as part of a complete education), a dancing master, and a few language masters who taught modern foreign languages.

Students from far and wide

Just as Groningen professors formed an international community, so Groningen students came from far and wide. Already from its first year, the University of Groningen was very attractive especially to students from German regions. In its inaugural year of 1614-1615, a total of 82 students appeared before the rector to be enrolled in the *album studiosorum*, and the first to do so was a German from

9. *Scepter of the beadle of the university, 1615. This scepter was always carried by the beadle when he led the professors to the auditorium of the university. On top of the scepter, the small figurine represents the goddess Athena (or Minerva). Clearly visible is also the coat of arms of the university.*

Hamm (in Westphalia) named Bernhard Sutholt. Many would follow in his foot-steps. In the period between 1614 and 1815 (a turning point in the university's history), approximately 12,000 students enrolled; of these, 4,533 (38%) came from abroad, meaning they were born outside the Republic. Most of these students enrolled in the 17th century: in its first one hundred years, the university welcomed no less than 3,430 international students! Note that the term 'international' here should be taken with a grain of salt. Most of these students came from principalities and cities in the northwest of what is now Germany, including Bremen, Bentheim and East Friesland. However, more remote cities and principalities also frequently provided the university with students, including Danzig, the Palatinate and Marburg. Together with students from Scandinavia, France, Scotland and even Hungary, the makeup of the student body was such that the University of Groningen had every right to call itself an international university.

The fact that Groningen (and the Dutch Republic in general) attracted so many German students was due to many different reasons, but one important reason was the political unrest in the German Empire. Shortly after the establishment of the University of Groningen, the Thirty Years' War broke out in Germany between the Catholic Emperor and a number of Protestant rulers. This led to recurring disruptions in university life in many German states. Many students were forced to leave their homelands (such as Heidelberg and Marburg) after they were conquered by Spanish or imperial troops, leading to Protestants being evicted from their universities. The same thing happened in France in the late 17th century, when King Louis XIV forced the Huguenots – the French Protestants – to convert to Catholicism and to close their institutions of higher education. Many Huguenots chose to emigrate instead, some of them settling in the Dutch

10. *View of the city of Groningen from the northwest, by Carl Christoff von Walwitz (1639). From the* liber amicorum *of the German student Friedrich Ludwig Helder. Von Walwitz studied law in Groningen from 1632.*

Republic. Of these, some came to Groningen to study or become professors. The political stability and well-known tolerance of the Republic in a turbulent Europe led to the University of Groningen becoming more international than it might otherwise have been.

In the 17th century, the students organized themselves according to their regions of origin: Groningen natives with other Groningen natives, Frisians with Frisians, and Gelderland natives with other Gelderland natives. International students followed this example. These student societies were known as '*nationes*', and the German 'nation' in particular was very strong. Student societies were not only formed for fun but also to help each other in times of struggle (illness, money problems) and to defend the students' common interests. If a professor was too harsh towards a student, the 'nation' to which the student belonged would intervene and stand up to the authorities, thus forcing the professor or the senate to review their judgment or release the student. The student world could be very rough at times.

Reason or revelation?

The University of Groningen fully participated in the great intellectual movements that swept across the Republic and the rest of Europe in the 17th century. The new philosophy of René Descartes was adopted early on in the Republic and also gained adepts in Groningen, leading to the same conflict between conservatives and innovators that was raging at other universities within the Republic around 1650. This conflict centred on the relationship between science and faith, or rather between reason and revelation. Upon their appointment, professors were required to sign the Reformed Church Creeds and were expected to adhere to the philosophy of the Greek philosopher Aristotle. But not all theologians and philosophers obeyed these instructions, which then caused tensions in Groningen.

From the moment Descartes published his brief *Discours de la méthode* in 1637, orthodox ministers and theologians accused him of undermining faith in God and paving the way for atheism with his methodological doubt and mechanistic natural philosophy. Ultimately, critics argued, such thinking would greatly damage the foundations of the state. Advocates of Cartesian philosophy, on the other hand, defended the freedom of philosophy and argued that the system of Descartes – who was himself far from being an atheist – was perfectly compatible with faith in the Divine, the immortal soul, and resurrection on the Day of Judgment. In Groningen, this view was shared by the professor of Greek and history, Tobias Andreae, and the theologian Samuel Maresius (who was also known as Samuel Desmarets).

26

11. *Tobias Andreae, professor of Greek, the most dedicated follower of René Descartes in Groningen. Engraving from Effigies et vitae (1654).*

At first it appeared as if Groningen would avoid becoming entangled in the conflict surrounding Descartes, but the university eventually did get caught up via an indirect route. Descartes' greatest opponent within the Republic was the Utrecht University theologian and professor Gisbertus Voetius. He asked one of his former pupils, Martin Schoock, the Groningen professor of classical languages and eloquence, to write a rebuttal of Descartes. The result was a short but sharply worded booklet ironically titled *Admiranda methodus* (1642), which combined serious criticism of Descartes with taunts that were in poor taste, even by the standards of the time. Descartes was very upset and brought a formal complaint against Schoock to the States of Groningen. An investigation was launched, which resulted in Schoock being reprimanded and Groningen Cartesians being

27

given free rein to teach their philosophy in their lectures, to the great vexation of Voetius. The typical Dutch policy of official constraints combined with de facto tolerance of controversial issues ensured that *libertas philosophandi* was reasonably safe in Groningen.

Incipient decline

The dispute over the big questions of the time did not make Groningen less attractive to students from the Republic and abroad, and students continued to enrol at a rate of one hundred or more each year. However, in the second half of the century, a decline set in which at first had nothing to do with relationships within the university but rather with the changing international political situation. In Germany, the Thirty Years' War had come to an end, which meant that German students could once again safely study in their homeland. Meanwhile, the Republic increasingly came under threat from surrounding countries. In 1665, the Bishop of Münster, Bernhard van Galen, invaded the eastern provinces, and Groningen was already preparing for a siege when the bishop was forced to relinquish his offensive. In 1672, he made a second attempt, this time with the support of French troops, resulting in a siege of the city. For a full month, Van Galen subjected Groningen to large-scale shelling offensives (which gave him his nickname '*Bommen Berend*', or Bombing Berend), but the city held on, in part thanks to the deployment of a student company repelling the enemy's attacks from the city walls. On 28 August 1672, the bishop was finally forced to abandon the siege, an event celebrated to this day. But the city being the centre of military hostilities was not good for the university.

12. *The Siege of Groningen, 1672 (detail). Etching by Jacob Harrewijn, 1684.*

The student company of 1672

The Bishop of Münster, Bernhard van Galen, began his siege of Groningen on 9 July 1672, by which time a special student company had already reported for duty to the provincial council to help defend the city. The company included Groningen natives but also students from the German borderlands, where the population was suffering at the hands of the Catholic bishop. The students were positioned at one of the most dangerous points in the defence lines, on the denuded lower part of the wall rising from the canal between Oosterpoort and Herepoort, on the southern side of the city. The professors tried to maintain some control over the students by issuing special regulations, which the students completely ignored. Everyone was astounded by the courage shown by the students during the offensive. At night they sang their own songs, loudly enough that the enemy troops on the other side of the canal could hear them. When one student was shot in the chest (he survived), his friends continued to sing the song 'Nightingale' so soldiers on the other side would not know they had hit their mark. And whenever the bishop came near the students, he was treated to a volley of insults. The whole thing may at times have been more reminiscent of a student party than a battlefield, but it kept the students' spirits up. And their tactic was rewarded: in early August, the odds shifted, and by the middle of the month, the bishop had been forced to abandon the siege. The students remained under arms until 8 November, when they were each awarded a silver badge of honour for their bravery and loyalty.

13. Banner of the company of students who helped to defend Groningen in 1672.

14. *Johann Bernoulli, professor of mathematics, 1695-1705. Engraving by J. Ruben (1743).*

The last quarter of the 17th century was also marked by a series of clashes among the university's theologians. Maresius, who had protected the Cartesians back in the 1640s, now became embroiled in a fierce conflict with his colleague Jacobus Alting. The conflict concerned the strict observance of the Sabbath, the God-appointed day of rest, an issue that may be difficult to understand today but one that played an important role at the time. Did the strict Sabbath rules only apply to Jews, on whom God had imposed them, or also to Christians, including the Republic's Reformed Protestants? The authorities who financed and governed the University of Groningen, the city of Groningen and the Ommelanden were all drawn into the conflict and forced to choose sides. This in turn led to ongoing disagreements on how to fill vacancies: the city tended to favour more liberal candidates than the Ommelanden, which meant that vacancies sometimes remained unfilled for years. As a result, in 1679, Groningen did not have a single theology professor.

From our modern-day perspective, the issues that led to discord may seem trivial. For example, Johann Bernoulli, a Swiss professor of mathematics and one of the founders of differential and integral calculus, found himself in trouble shortly after his appointment in 1695 for pointing out in his lectures that the human body is continuously renewed through the process of metabolism. The body of today, he claimed, is not the same as that of yesterday. His colleague, the theologian Paulus Hulsius, found this highly problematic, since it raised the question of which body would be brought back to life on Resurrection Day: the body of today or that of yesterday (or the day before)? This conflict was fought out in the form of disputations in which professors had their students defend and attack their theses. The conflict was never clearly resolved, but the controversy did not improve the university's reputation.

Shortly afterwards, Bernoulli found himself in trouble once again for introducing Groningen to experimental philosophy, in which philosophical or scientific theses were supported by experiments. From the start, Groningen theologians were against this new form of philosophical enquiry. According to the long-standing philosophy of Aristotle, which they still adhered to, experiments forced nature to yield answers and were therefore unreliable as a source of knowledge. Since Bernoulli had no laboratory of his own, he carried out these physics experiments in 1698 in the Martinikerk, which also hit a nerve with the theologians, who saw it as a desecration of a place of worship. All of this led to Bernoulli gladly leaving Groningen after being offered a position as university professor in his native Basel in 1705. And so it came to be that the University of Groningen lost the professor with the most international allure and significance it had had in the first century of its existence.

Bernoulli was not the only professor to leave Groningen, and since the city of Groningen and the Ommelanden often disagreed on how to fill vacancies, the number of lecturers dropped dramatically, as did the number of students. By 1713, the university had only five professors and 23 newly enrolled students.

2

15. *Anatomical lesson
of Petrus Camper
(right), city surgeon
in Amsterdam and
professor of anatomy
in Groningen. Paint-
ing by Tibout Regters
(1758).*

Enlightenment, but in moderation (1714-1814)

By 1714, the University of Groningen was in such a deplorable state that the authorities decided not to celebrate the university's first centenary. And yet, not for the last time in its history, the university showed proof of great resilience in its second century in existence. By appointing many 'enlightened' professors, Groningen even managed to overtake Franeker on the virtual ranking of Dutch universities and to rightfully claim the title of the most important northern university. However, the Enlightenment, so popular in Groningen, also had its limits, as more than one professor was to discover.

Enlightened minds

When the last professor in the Faculty of Law died in 1716, the States-General finally took action and decided to appoint no less than five new professors. This gave the university a new élan. Soon enrolments were once again up to 60 a year – not as many as in the mid-17th century but enough to allow the university to once again function normally. It would have been unrealistic for the university to expect to match its 17th-century heyday, since international students were no longer forced or willing to come to the Republic in such large numbers. What's more, the university now had to compete with other forms of higher education throughout Europe that were more tailored to practical life and therefore very popular.

One of Groningen's new professors was the jurist Jean Barbeyrac, an outspoken representative of the early Enlightenment in Europe. Barbeyrac was appointed professor in Lausanne, a Protestant university that increasingly suffered from the intolerance of the Swiss Reformed community, which demanded strict adherence to the Reformed Church Creeds. Barbeyrac was prepared to sign the creeds but only 'to the extent that they were consistent with the Bible', which was not good enough for the orthodox authorities. Although Groningen was also Prot-

JOANNES BARBEYRACIUS
J.U.D. & PUBLICI PRIVATIQUE
JURIS ANTECESSOR IN ACADEMIA
GRONINGO-OMLAND REGIÆQUE
SOCIETATIS BEROLIN. SOCIUS.
Natus Biterris die 15.
Martii M.DC.LXXIV.

estant, Barbeyrac believed the Dutch Republic to be more tolerant than Switzerland. And he was right: he enjoyed the full support of the city magistrates and provincial nobility who protected him against attacks from strict Calvinists. This allowed Barbeyrac to fully focus on European academia. He became a great advocate of intellectual and religious freedom and tolerance based on natural law. He believed that reason, not faith, dictated what was morally responsible and that education would allow all people to act morally and find happiness. His own primary contribution to the Enlightenment programme was the translation into French – alongside his own comments – of classic texts on natural law such as the famous *De iure belli ac pacis* by the Dutch jurist Hugo de Groot. He was also

the editor of the international journal *Bibliothèque raissonée des ouvrages des savans de l'Europe*, an important communication channel for European scholars. It was also thanks to the cosmopolitan Barbeyrac that in 1722 Groningen welcomed another Swiss professor, Nicolas de Crousaz, who definitively introduced to Groningen the modern experimental approach to natural philosophy.

The position of the University of Groningen was strengthened even further by a state revolution in the mid-18th century. An unlucky war against France led to a growing popular movement in the Republic of the United Netherlands that gave Stadtholder William IV far more power than previously. From 1748 onwards, the Republic started to resemble a monarchy. In the Province of Groningen, a new administrative regulation was introduced – the Reformatory Regulation – which led to the Stadtholder gaining complete jurisdiction over the university. From this point onwards, the Stadtholder was both head of the board of curators and *rector magnificentissimus*. All decisions, including those concerning appointments, had to be approved by him. This turned out to be quite beneficial for the University of Groningen. The tension between the city of Groningen and the Ommelanden could no longer paralyse the university's normal operations or block new investments, as it had done around 1700. For example, Anna van Hannover, widow of William IV (who had died in 1749) and guardian of the still

17. The ceremonial bowl of the learned society Pro Excolendo Jure Patrio, *around 1770.*

underage William V, appointed no less than seven new professors, some of whom went on to become very famous.

Thanks to this new impulse, Groningen once again grew, while its competitor Franeker slipped further into obscurity. Whereas in the 17th century, Franeker had clearly been the country's second university after Leiden, in the 18th century it could no longer maintain this status. As a result, the originally smaller Groningen became the academic metropolis of the north. This was largely due to some disastrous budget cuts in Franeker but also to the liveliness of Groningen as a city. Franeker was a small, quiet town without much in the way of social life beyond its university, while Groningen was a provincial capital, a relatively large city with a flourishing cultural and social life. This is illustrated by the fact that, more or less simultaneously with cities in the west of the country, Groningen acquired its own scholarly society in which professors and educated citizens met on an equal footing to discuss the newest scientific developments. Officially, this society, called *Pro Excolendo Jure Patrio*, focused on law, but since the debate included any factors that affected the legal system – from history and geology to the climate – it ultimately grew into a very broad-minded society that was in principle open to all scholars. No such thing existed in Franeker.

The limits of the Enlightenment

While Franeker grew quieter, the Groningen administrators showed their willingness to invest in modern developments. Ambitious young scholars but also established scientists felt at home in the city – people such as Wouter van Doeveren, who was appointed professor of medicine in 1753 and went on to become a famous obstetrician and anatomist. He was a great advocate of vaccination against the pox, even in the face of fierce resistance from more conservative physicians and concerned church ministers (who believed that deliberately making people slightly ill – which is what vaccinations usually do – went against the divine order). Another clearly modern scholar was the German jurist Frederik Adolf van der Marck, who was appointed professor of constitutional, natural and domestic law and Roman law in 1758. Van der Marck broke with the tradition of only teaching Roman law, which enjoyed high regard but had no use in legal practice. Instead, he gave lectures in local law, the legislation the future lawyers had to work with. Van der Marck was extremely popular among students.

The most important Groningen professor in the second half of the 18th century was the anatomist Petrus Camper. Camper was already a professor in Franeker and Amsterdam (where a college without *ius promovendi* had been established in 1632) when he accepted the invitation to take over the chair in anatomy in Groningen in 1763, alongside Van Doeveren. Camper was a master of anatomy: he made excellent drawings and was considered an expert artist (he also advised in the construction of Groningen's new city hall). He also wrote provocative essays in new cultural journals opposing slavery and women's subordination. Camper was responsible for introducing comparative anatomy to Groningen. He is famous for comparing facial lines in apes and various human races, a comparison that was regrettably later used by racists to justify the dominant position of the white race. He also involved his students in his work at the surgery clinic he founded. Finally, he supported Van Doeveren in his campaign for vaccination against the pox and created a society for combatting the cattle plague that frequently affected the northern Netherlands with a vaccination programme.

But Camper also faced the limits of the Enlightenment. In 1772, Van der Marck found himself in trouble when he and his students went too far in provoking the Groningen ministers, who responded by accusing him of making claims in his teachings and publications that opposed the Church Creeds he had sworn allegiance to upon his appointment. The ministers insisted that the Stadtholder dismiss Van der Marck. Although Camper was a liberal himself and would have been

18. Bust of Petrus Camper, professor of anatomy, by the French sculptor Marie-Anne Falconet-Collot, 1781. Camper inoculated the daughter of the artist and thus saved the child's life. By making this bust, the artist wanted to express her gratitude to Camper.

Camper on blacks and slaves

Petrus Camper was not only a great scholar, equal to the great Herman Boerhaave; he was also an enlightened man, something he frequently demonstrated in his public lectures at the anatomical theatre in the Broerkerk choir. These lectures drew great numbers of students and Groningen citizens and were often published in cultural journals. On 14 November 1764, Camper held a lecture entitled 'On the Origin and Colour of Blacks', published in 1772 in the journal *De Rhapsodist*. Based on a few well-chosen anatomical specimens (including the corpse of an Angolan boy, some skin from the arm of an Italian sailor, and a white woman's breast), he demonstrated that there was no anatomical difference between a black and a white person, or between a man and a woman. The only difference was skin colour, an effect that could be attributed to climate and geographical circumstances. Camper therefore concluded that 'we are all black to some extent'. And in case they had not fully understood him, he addressed his audience directly: 'We are all but white Moors.' It is therefore no surprise that Camper was a staunch opponent of slavery. In 1769, in the journal *De Philosooph*, he harshly denounced the slave trade, in which the Dutch also took part: 'We too, no matter how much we pretend to be great Christians, take part in this barbaric trade in America and elsewhere and for financial gain subjugate human beings who by the laws of nature have as much right to freedom as we do.'

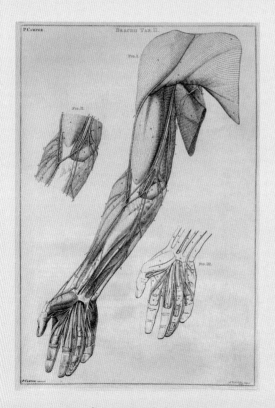

19. *Anatomy of an arm, from Petrus Camper,* Demonstrationum anatomico-pathologicarum liber primus *(Amsterdam 1760-1762).*

all too glad to see the Church lose its hold on intellectual life within and outside the university, at the crucial moment he supported the conservatives who called for the dismissal of Van der Marck. He did so to protect his own position and especially not to harm his political aspirations. Through his marriage to the daughter of a Frisian Regent, Camper had become a wealthy man, and his ownership of land led him to become involved in Frisian politics. Because of this, he was forced to manoeuvre within the boundaries allowed by the Stadtholder's supporters. In 1773, Van der Marck was dismissed with Camper's support, but this made Camper's position so difficult that in the same year he gave up his chair and retired to his Frisian estate as a private scholar.

The Van der Marck affair left deep marks on Groningen university life in the last quarter of the 18th century. This may explain why, during the Time of the Patriots (1784-1787), when a group of dissatisfied magistrates and citizens revolted against the Stadtholder's rule and demanded democratic reforms, Groningen kept quiet, unlike Franeker, where many professors took the Patriots' side. As a consequence, when the old order was restored, many Franeker professors were

20. *Petrus Driessen, professor of medicine and chemistry, by Wessel Lubbers, around 1820.*

21. *Georges Cuvier, engraving by John Thomson, around 1800. In 1811, the zoologist Cuvier was commissioned by the French emperor Napoleon to inspect the institutions of higher education in the former Kingdom of Holland, then annexed by the French empire. Cuvier advised the emperor to incorporate the University of Groningen in the system of the Imperial University, while at the same time closing down the University of Franeker.*

dismissed, a blow the Frisian university never recovered from. During this period, for the first time, there were more Frisian students in Groningen than in Franeker. Incidentally, Groningen also faced dwindling student numbers. And yet the political restoration did not lead to the University of Groningen becoming more conservative. On the contrary, this was the period in which Curator Antony Adriaan van Iddekinge, the university's strongman and right-hand man of the Stadtholder, helped a highly promising student of medicine, Petrus Driessen, to explore modern developments in chemistry abroad before returning to Groningen as a professor in 1787. In line with the Enlightenment's virtue of usefulness, Driessen aimed to apply chemistry – previously viewed as no more than an auxiliary subject in medicine – to industry and agriculture.

State and university

The French Revolution of 1789 heralded the end of the Republic of the Seven United Netherlands. In 1795, French troops 'freed' the Republic, and the Stadtholder fled to England. In 1796, a truly representative parliament, the National

Assembly, met for the first time in The Hague. Its most important task was to formulate a constitution for the new nation, with attention given to a higher education system. The prevailing idea was that an end had to be made to the division and particularism that had marked the Republic. No longer would each province be allowed its own university, each one too small to compete internationally. Rather than the country having too many universities, the idea was for higher education to be focused in a single institution that would be so generously financed as to be able to compete with large universities abroad. For the first time, Groningen was confronted with national policy on higher education formulated by a central government in The Hague. It was generally assumed that the national university would be located in Leiden, the oldest university and also the one with the most students and professors. Other cities would at most be allowed to offer preparatory programmes for the national university. This would have resulted in the closure of these younger universities, including Groningen, which explains why the proposal met with sharp criticism. Universities argued that the geographical dispersion of higher education had always been characteristic of the Dutch educational system. Their main arguments were that it was unfair to force all students to move to the western town of Leiden (since this would make studying a lot more expensive for a student from Groningen than for a student from, say, The Hague) and that universities had an important role to play as cultural centres in their own regions.

In the end, the rigorous concentration and centralization envisaged by the new rulers in The Hague came to nought. A series of coups and the ongoing controversy surrounding the constitution prevented any radical changes from being implemented for the time being. This did not stop the University of Groningen from introducing innovations where needed. For example, in 1797, the physician Evert Jan Thomassen à Thuessink turned an old orphanage into an academic hospital that admitted patients on the basis of their potential role in education. In 1803, the hospital relocated to a complex in the southwestern part of the city (the present-day Munnekeholm).

It was only under the rule of Emperor Napoleon that fundamental changes were implemented. In 1806, the Emperor appointed his brother, Louis Napoleon, as monarch of the Kingdom of Holland, only to change his mind four years later and annex the territory of the Former Republic, dismissing Louis Napoleon. This time, serious change was on its way. In the spring of 1811, the Emperor sent two envoys to the new territory to report on the state of the universities. The idea was to reduce the number of universities per *arrondissement* back to one or perhaps two, as had been done elsewhere throughout the Empire. The envoys travelled around the country, visited all of the universities and finally submitted a report in which they advised the retaining of two universities: Leiden and Groningen.

41

The most important reason for retaining Groningen alongside Leiden was the fact that the Dutch were keen to send their children to study close to home, and in the winter the connections between Holland and the north were particularly difficult (in those days the north of the country was separated from Holland by the Zuiderzee). The Emperor followed this advice. In October 1811, he decreed that Leiden and Groningen would be the only universities included in the imperial university system which had its headquarters in Paris (at the time, therefore, Dutch universities fell under the jurisdiction of Paris). The University of Utrecht was demoted to an 'école secundaire', while Franeker was not even mentioned. This was cause for celebration in Groningen, while the Franeker scholars mourned.

3

GRONINGEN   Mineral Geologisch Laboratorium

22. *The Mineralogical and
Geological Institute of
professor F.J.P. van Calker,
1901. The building was soon
popularly known as 'The
Castle' (Het Kasteel).*

A century of extremes (1814-1914)

T he University of Groningen was not subject to the French regime for very long. Following a failed invasion of Russia (1812), Napoleon's star faded fast and by late 1813, Russian troops had driven him out of his Dutch territories. This led to a major overhaul of the political and academic landscape. The Netherlands became a monarchy, and the provinces definitively lost control of their universities. From this point onwards, the University of Groningen was part of a national higher education system governed by The Hague. Over the course of the 19th century, this had both positive and negative effects, as periods of threat and deep crisis alternated with some spectacular periods of flourishing.

A new beginning

After the French were driven out, authority fell back into the hands of the Stadtholder – this time the son of former Stadtholder William V, William Frederick, who as King William I took over command of the Southern Netherlands (modern-day Belgium) with the help of the Allied troops in 1814. In the new Kingdom of the Netherlands, a committee led by the nobleman Frans-Adam van der Duyn van Maasdam designed a new regulation for universities, aiming to combine all the strong aspects of the old system (from before 1795) with the advantages of the French system. This new regulation, which in practice only applied to the Northern Netherlands (approximately corresponding to the territory of the former Republic), resulted in what was known as the Organic Decree in August 1815. The University of Groningen had every reason to look to the future with confidence, having a year earlier celebrated its second centenary in splendour in the presence of the King. The academic Senate met for a formal session, popular festivities were organized, and the entire city was decorated with flags and banners.

According to the Organic Decree, the Northern Netherlands was to have three universities: Leiden, Groningen and Utrecht, now all financed by the national government and therefore called Rijkshogescholen, later Rijksuniversiteiten. Franeker had hoped for a revival but was instead demoted to a *Rijksathenaeum*, an institution of higher education without *ius promovendi* and one that was only allowed to teach preparatory university courses. Every university, including Groningen, was to consist of five faculties, while the Faculty of Literature and Philosophy was split according to the French model into a Faculty of Arts and Philosophy and a Faculty of Mathematics and Physics (which mostly served as preparation for the Faculty of Medicine).

Any exclusive link to a single religious denomination was abolished, and professors were no longer required to subscribe to the Reformed Church Creeds. At least in theory, the universities had become secular rather than religious institutions. This led to a debate as early as 1795 on whether there was still room at the university for a theological faculty that only served one denomination, the Reformed Church. However, as other arrangements turned out to be untenable – the Catholic Church wished to retain control of its own priest training rather than relinquish it to the universities – nothing changed. The Organic Decree also described in great detail how many professors were to teach at each of the universities and in what subjects (Leiden was awarded more professors than Groningen and Utrecht and paid theirs better). All universities also started teaching new subjects, including agronomy (agricultural science) and Dutch language and literature. Clear entry requirements were established, and degree programmes were divided into a general *propedeuse*, then a broad candidate phase and finally a specialized doctoral phase, with the option of completing a PhD dissertation that entitled graduates to exercise a given profession such as physician, lawyer or teacher. National entry and examination fees were introduced, but course tuition fees were still paid directly to the professors.

A point of principle was the stipulation that courses would continue to be taught in Latin, as during the days of the Republic. In the course of the 18th century, it had increasingly become customary for European universities to teach in their national languages, but the Van der Duyn van Maasdam committee retained Latin as the language to be used at universities, partly out of conservatism and partly in the hope that this would once again attract international students to the Dutch universities. The number of international students in the Republic had dwindled throughout the 18th century, and in the early 19th century there was only a group of East Frisian students who were in Groningen to study theology. This was due to the fact that East Friesland was partially Reformed and the closest Protestant university was in Groningen. It was, however, a vain hope to think that teaching in Latin would once again attract international students. Nationalism in higher education had already suppressed Latin as the language of learning and science throughout Europe, and this was in practice soon to be the case in the Netherlands as well.

Usefulness and virtue

After the publication of the Organic Decree, the University of Groningen went through yet another period of moderate prosperity. The number of first-year students grew to a viable 60 a year (so that approximately 250 to 300 students could be found in Groningen every year), and the university enjoyed a buoyant academic life. The greatest drive behind this revival was Theodorus van Swinderen, who was appointed professor of natural history in 1814 and who had already played an active role in stimulating university life in his role as school inspector during the French era. Van Swinderen was more of an organizer than a scholar. In 1801, while still a student, he had founded the Physical and Chemical Society, later renamed the Physical Society, which more or less functioned as the research department of the University of Groningen in the 19th century. Van Swinderen put

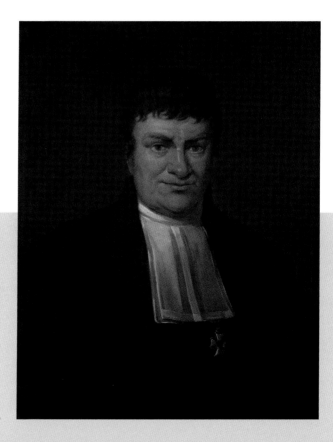

23. *Theodorus van Swinderen, by Jan Ensing (1843). Van Swinderen was professor of natural history (1814-1851) and one of the founders of the Physical and Chemical Society.*

together a lavishly furnished natural history cabinet, as the Organic Decree mandated every university to do. In 1820, this cabinet was greatly enriched thanks to the donation of the extended natural history collection created by Petrus Camper on his Frisian estate, which the King purchased on the university's behalf. Van Swinderen embodied, like no other, late 18th-century Enlightened Christianity, in which usefulness and virtue went hand in hand. Everything he did was aimed at educating students to become valuable and virtuous citizens.

The same enlightened ideals also led Groningen students to unite in a student society called Vindicat atque Polit (Upholds and Civilizes). Following the disappearance of the *nationes* in the course of the 18th century, the student world had become fragmented. There were active friend and study groups, but these were not of a lasting nature. The most important of these groups were *ontgroensenaten*, self-appointed boards that submitted new students to hazing practices aimed to bring them to heel. These hazing practices were at times brutal, leading in 1815 to a few Groningen students forming a general senate intended to regulate 'wild' hazing practices. This senate saw itself as *the* representative of the student body and had a dual objective: safeguarding the rights of students and implementing a kind of civilizing offensive to refine the students' more coarse behaviour. The new senate quickly acquired the character of a student society, with its own laws and meeting place (called Mutua Fides). All students were free to pay the enrolment fee and join Vindicat, and in practice nearly all of them did. Vindicat was the first student society in the Netherlands, although other universities quickly followed suit.

The focus on usefulness also characterized the work of the most important scholar of the Physical Society: the apothecary and chemist Sibrandus Stratingh, who followed in Petrus Driessen's footsteps and was appointed professor of chemistry in 1824. Stratingh did not develop any great original theories, but he was extremely well informed about any research done abroad and applied the results in an inventive manner in his own research. He improved the preparation of medicines, actively contributed to combatting infectious diseases and experimented with a self-propelled steam-driven vehicle. In the last years of his life (he died in 1841), he even worked on an electric vehicle, a precursor of the electric car. Usefulness was also a leitmotif in the work of the botanist Herman Christiaan van Hall, who in 1840 founded an agronomy school in the neighbouring village of Haren, where practical courses on agricultural methods were taught.

The first electric car

Professor Sibrandus Stratingh was one of the first – if not the first – to build an electrically driven vehicle together with his technical assistant Christopher Becker in what was a precursor of the electric car. During a meeting of the Physical and Chemical Society in Groningen on 4 November 1835, he offered a demonstration of the vehicle, an event that was reported by the *Groninger Courant* two days later. The news travelled fast across Europe via other newspapers and journals in the Netherlands and abroad. At the time, Stratingh was building steam engines, and one of his steam vehicles had already been test driven. But when he read that a mechanical engineer in faraway Koningsbergen (modern-day Kaliningrad) had invented an engine that used electricity to bring engine parts in motion, he decided to create a vehicle using an improved version of this engine instead of the cumbersome, dangerous and heavy steam engine. This 'electromagnetic automobile' did not go beyond the scale-model stage, but Stratingh can still claim to be the inventor of the electric car. An improved version of Stratingh's scale model can be seen at the University Museum in Groningen. Once owned by the Physical Society, it was purchased by the university in 1934. Groningen Nobel Laureate Ben Feringa, known for his research on the nano-engine, donated a similar model of Stratingh's electric car to the Nobel Museum in Stockholm, as homage to an inspiring predecessor.

24. *Electrical car devised by Sibrandus Stratingh, professor of chemistry, 1824-1841.*

25. Petrus Hofstede de Groot, by J.H. Egenberger, around 1885. Hofstede de Groot was professor of theology from 1829 to 1872.

Academic freedom

In the first half of the 19th century, the University of Groningen became famous for being the birthplace of a new theological movement within the Reformed Church: Groningen Theology. It was led by Petrus Hofstede de Groot, professor of theology, together with his colleagues Johan Frederik van Oordt and Louis Gerlach Pareau. Hofstede de Groot thought little of the dogmatic Reformed Church life in the Netherlands. He believed that history showed a gradual growth in religious awareness and that dogmas and creeds were only temporary embodiments of this process. This was directly opposed to a movement known as Réveil, which aimed to bring about a renewal of religious faith through strict adherence to the old 16th and 17th-century creeds (incidentally, Hofstede de Groot heartily agreed that there was a crisis in religious awareness). Caught between these two movements, the Reformed Church found itself embroiled in a bitter struggle throughout the 1830s and 1840s as both movements attempted to convince the moderate majority in the General Synod – the highest governing body of the Reformed Church – to take their side.

The conflict between Hofstede de Groot and Réveil supporters went beyond theological matters. In the mid-1840s, Réveil supporters tried to convince the Synod to put an end to the influence of Hofstede de Groot and his ilk. They proposed to have all Dutch theology professors sign a statement in which they swore unconditional allegiance to the Reformed Church Creeds. Although professors had not been required to sign these creeds since 1811, theology professors were responsible for training Reformed Church ministers, and the orthodox faction considered it only proper that they should sign such a statement. Hofstede de Groot and his supporters vehemently opposed the idea. Their main argument was that as professors, and therefore researchers, they had to have complete freedom in the topics they wished to investigate and teach to their students. They claimed that the entire Reformation movement since Luther had been based on free academic research and that the Protestant Churches were betraying their own principles by trying to abolish this freedom. In the end, Hofstede de Groot posited, history showed that this kind of freedom consistently benefitted the people and the Church. Academic researchers should therefore not be subject to violence done to the conscience, even if their teaching or research might sometimes cause discomfort. This made Hofstede de Groot the first person in the Netherlands to formulate the principle of academic freedom, which remains one of the central values of university life to this day.

Threatened with closure

While Hofstede de Groot was battling with the orthodox faction of the Reformed Church, the University of Groningen as a whole was also facing a crisis. The union of the Northern and Southern Netherlands under King William I was not a success, and in 1830 the southern provinces seceded, forming the new Kingdom of Belgium. William I refused to accept this and in 1831 sent his troops south to call the 'Belgians' to order. This military expedition also involved volunteers, including a battalion of students from various cities – the Volunteer Flankers Battalion – which accompanied the regular troops but were not required to fight. Nonetheless, the Groningen flankers were hailed as heroes upon their return from the front in November 1831. The expedition was a military success, but the Great Powers (England and France) forced William I to recall his troops, and Belgium became de facto independent. Nonetheless, the King refused to accept defeat and even though he finally complied in 1839, he kept a large and expensive army at the ready. As a result, as early as 1836, Dutch universities suffered severe budget cuts. For example, the number of grants for children of less wealthy parents were substantially curbed. In 1840, when the Belgian question was finally resolved, it became clear that the Netherlands was suffering from a severe financial deficit that could only be remedied through drastic budget cuts. One way to achieve this was to close down one or two universities. As the smallest of the three national universities, Groningen was the obvious candidate.

Hofstede de Groot immediately set to work to defend 'his' university. He demonstrated that concentrating higher education within one or at most two universities would not lead to any real savings. He also argued that this kind of centralization ran against the nature of the Dutch, who wanted education to be equally distributed across the country, and he warned the government that the one remaining large university could easily turn into a hotbed of revolutionary student agitation, as it had in Germany. Smaller universities meant that the authorities had better insight into what was going on among students and were able to intervene earlier. These arguments proved to be effective. Groningen was not closed down and was allowed to keep all its faculties; instead, the *Rijksathenaeum* in Franeker, which had been ailing for some time, was formally disbanded in 1843.

26. *Standard bearer of Volunteer Flankers Battalion from Groningen during the Ten Days Campaign against the revolting Belgians, 1831.*

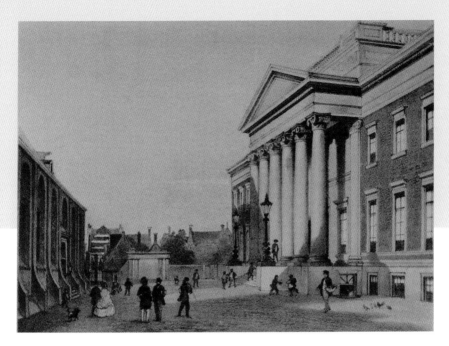

27. The Academy Building in 1850, opposite the former Academy Church, by C.C.A. Last.

This did not, however, mean that the University of Groningen had averted all threats to its existence. The danger lay in a slow decline in enrolment numbers. While until 1840, approximately 60 new students had enrolled every year, a decade later this figure had dropped to 50, and it continued to drop further still. This made it easier for those who wanted to close the University of Groningen to argue their case. Such proposals were often voiced by the liberal faction, who had come to power in 1848 following a series of revolutions in Europe and the Netherlands. The liberal government's strongman, Johan Rudolf Thorbecke, was known for his penchant for economizing and for his distaste for provincial particularism, which he believed – not altogether wrongly – to be alive at the University of Groningen. Groningen had little to hope for and much to fear from Thorbecke.

Crisis but no collapse

Contemporaries undoubtedly must have wondered why increasingly fewer students were finding their way to Groningen. Was it due to the austerity of a central government that was far more generous towards the other two universities?

28. The new University Library, built in 1864, by Ferdinand van Wolde, 1912.

Or were Groningen professors to blame for their rather conservative ideas and refusal to keep up with the times, such that the university was increasingly becoming alienated from the liberal bourgeoisie? Had the moderate revival of the first decades of the century given way to stagnation and collapse?

There were as yet no signs of collapse. In the mid-19th century, Groningen was still home to many inspiring and innovative professors, including the physiologist Izaac van Deen (the first Dutch professor of Jewish origin), the Dutch language and literature expert Matthias de Vries, the jurists Cornelis Star Numan and Bernard Jan Gratama, the chemist Petrus Johannes van Kerckhoff and the physician Samuel Sigmund Rosenstein. Furthermore, the university's facilities were modernized on a regular basis, starting with a new, classical-style Academy Building built on the location of the former Sywen Convent, which had become dilapidated over the years and lacked an auditorium in which to hold inaugural lectures and PhD defences. The Broerkerk across the street from the Academy Building had functioned as an auditorium (the Aula), but in 1829 William I returned the building to the Roman Catholic Church. All of this undermined the university's image, which was one of the reasons the city of Groningen decided to use its own funds to build a new home for the university when the national government refused to loosen its purse strings. The construction of the new Academy Building, officially opened in 1850, once again emphasized the close connection between the university and the city (and the province), despite the fact that the former was now officially a national institution. Two years later, the university once again had reason for a modest celebration when the renovation of the academic hospital on the Munnekeholm was completed. The new hospital was funded jointly by the province, the city and the national government and acted not only as an academic hospital but also as a provincial and city hospital. Later on, a new library building was added (just in time for the celebration of the university's 250th anniversary in 1864), together with an ultramodern physiology laboratory behind the Academy Building. Yet another sign that the University of Groningen was far from declining was the fact that in 1871 it opened its doors to Aletta Jacobs, the first female Dutch student. In Groningen liberal circles, there was a surprising openness to women's participation in social life and broad support for their right to education.

A factor that did negatively affect the University of Groningen was the process of Dutch national unification. In the unified state that the Netherlands had become, the west was the political, economic and cultural centre of the country, and it increasingly drew in people from the periphery. This was further facilitated by the creation of a railway network that primarily made the west more easily accessible: in 1870, a direct line connecting Groningen to the west was opened. Prospective students who lived in the provinces between Groningen and the west of the country, who might have previously chosen to study in Groningen, now opted for Leiden or Utrecht. In addition, around the middle of the century, the small influx of students from across the German border dried up completely. Groningen increasingly had to rely on students from its immediate vicinity, which in the long term would not be enough.

Rescue

Around 1868, as serious attempts were made to formulate a new law on higher education, Groningen's prospects seemed rather bleak: there were only 150 students left in Groningen! Draft versions of the new law – which was repeatedly withdrawn and resubmitted due to repeated changes of government – did specify that all three national universities would be maintained, but the arguments for this position were rather weak. The House of Representatives suspected that the Minister of Home Affairs secretly hoped for an amendment to close one of the universities, namely Groningen. In Groningen, the professors, the students, well-to-do citizens, the press – everyone – jumped into action, but closure still seemed unavoidable. And yet it did not happen. MPs from the northern part of the country made a deal with their colleagues from the province of Holland who were keen to grant the municipality of Amsterdam permission to turn their athenaeum into a full-fledged municipally funded university. As a result, there

Aletta Jacobs, the Netherlands' first female student

Aletta Jacobs (1854-1929) was the daughter of a Jewish country doctor from the Groningen city of Sappemeer. After training as an apothecary assistant, in 1871 she expressed the wish to study medicine. There was nothing in the law to forbid this. In 1815, it had been so self-evident that only young men would study that women had not been formerly excluded, although common opinion had it that women were unsuited for academia. However, Thorbecke, who as Minister of Home Affairs was in charge of the universities, wrote to Aletta's father that she was allowed to follow lectures and participate in practicals, having satisfied himself that the candidate student's intentions were serious. A year later, he also granted her permission to sit the propaedeutic medical examination (a decision he signed on his deathbed). Contrary to what some feared, this did not lead to dozens of female students enrolling in Jacobs' wake, but the unspoken taboo had now been broken. Aletta Jacobs graduated from the University of Groningen in 1879. After a study period in London, where she came into contact with the modern women's movement, she established herself as the first Dutch female physician in Amsterdam. She became a great advocate of women's rights, including the right to vote. She was president of the Association for Women's Suffrage and played an active role in the International Woman Suffrage Alliance. During the First World War, she devoted herself to peace and even travelled to the US to plead with President Wilson for mediation by neutral states. Groningen did not forget Aletta Jacobs. Her bust stands in front of the Harmonie Building, and a biennial Aletta Jacobs Prize is awarded to women who distinguish themselves in promoting women's emancipation.

29. *Bronze bust of Aletta Jacobs on the square before the Harmony Building, by Theresia van der Pant (1990).*

was no parliamentary majority to support the closure of Groningen, and the provision that national universities would be maintained in Leiden, Utrecht and Groningen was passed in the House of Representatives without further discussion. This led to the bizarre situation that a law originally intended to reduce the number of universities from three to two instead made it possible to increase that number to four. In any event, when the new law – which included various provisions to guarantee better facilities for universities – finally passed in April 1876, Groningen was able to sigh with relief and look to the future with renewed optimism.

Dawn of a second Golden Age

The new law also stipulated that Latin would no longer be the language of academic life: from this point onwards, neither lectures nor official documents had to be drafted in Latin. In practice, Dutch had already largely replaced Latin, but the former now became the official language. The University of Groningen was now a truly *Dutch* university, where Dutch teachers taught almost exclusively Dutch students in Dutch. This did not mean that the university had become disconnected from general developments in science and research. The last quarter of the 19th century and the first decade of the 20th century were a veritable scientific heyday, and contemporaries spoke of a 'second Golden Age' comparable to the first Golden Age of the 17th century.

The new higher education act came at exactly the right time for Groningen. In the last quarter of the 19th century, the city of Groningen had grown tremendously and become a dynamic northern metropolis. From 1870 to 1910, the population doubled from 40,000 to nearly 80,000 (compared to 570,000 inhabitants in Amsterdam, the largest city in the Netherlands, in 1910). Due to changes in how the Netherlands protected itself against potential external attackers (i.e. Germany), the fortifications surrounding Groningen were no longer required and the fortresses constricting the city could be pulled down. The newly available land was used to build prestigious houses surrounded by greenery, and outside the old city walls new residential districts were created for workers and citizens. Groningen became more attractive as a student city, and this translated into a gradual increase in student numbers. Whereas Groningen had a maximum of 150 students around 1870, by 1890 this number had increased to 415 and by 1913 to 611. The new law also expanded the subjects taught at universities to include disciplines such as pharmaceutical science, geology and mineralogy, and it made certain specializations more autonomous, such as astronomy and social medicine, which also led to an increase in the number of professors from 22 to 32. Groningen was still only slightly larger than the smallest German university at the time (Rostock),

57

but within the Netherlands it was bridging the gap with Leiden and Utrecht. And this was only the beginning. In the 1880s, for example, Groningen became the first Dutch university to offer higher education in modern languages, which once again required the appointment of new professors, starting with Barend Sijmons, who was appointed professor of German in 1881.

The new law brought other changes, too. For example, it stipulated that tuition fees were to be paid directly to the government rather than to professors, which drastically changed the relationship between student and professor. In addition, the university's general propaedeutic phase shifted to preparatory higher and secondary education. Traditionally, the gymnasium had been the only institution granting access to university, but it became increasingly unclear why knowledge of Greek and Latin was required for all university subjects. As a result, pupils from what was known as the *Hogere Burgerschool* (Higher Burgher School) or HBS (founded in 1863 by Thorbecke with a curriculum heavily focused on modern languages, mathematics and science) increasingly found their way to university. Perhaps the most important change was the fact that scientific research became one of the university's core tasks alongside teaching. In the new definition of higher education, research was even given priority: 'Higher education

30. The Physical Laboratory, around 1910. The neo-gothic style in which this building was erected is typical for laboratories built in the late 19th and early 20th century.

31. *Jacobus Cornelius Kapteyn, professor of astronomy, and his wife during their first visit to Mount Wilson Observatory, Pasadena, CA., 1908. In that year, Kapteyn was appointed research assistant at the Observatory, but as there was no lodging on top of the mountain, he had to stay in a tent. Later a special cottage was built for Kapteyn, the Kapteyn Cottage.*

Kapteyn: the astronomer without an observatory

O ne structure notably missing from the list of new university buildings was an astronomical observatory. Although the new professor of astronomy, Jacobus Cornelius Kapteyn (1851-1922), repeatedly asked for one to be built, the government kept waiving his requests until Kapteyn eventually gave up. He focused instead on processing photographic data collected by other researchers. He then collaborated with a British astronomer in South Africa, David Gill, who had created a photographic map of the southern hemisphere but was unable to process the data himself. Gill sent his photographic plates to Groningen, where Kapteyn completed all the measurements with one or two assistants in his 'astronomical laboratory' and organized the data into tables. Based on Gill's data, Kapteyn published the *Cape Photographic Durchmusterung* (1896-1900), a work that brought him international fame. Based on the data, Kapteyn went on to formulate a theory about cosmic stellar streams and a model of the Milky Way including the sun and the earth. This granted him not only membership in international scholarly associations and a number of prestigious medals but also an invitation in 1908 to spend part of every year working as an associate researcher at Mt Wilson in California, home to the world's largest reflector telescope at the time. There, under much better climatological conditions than in the damp and misty Netherlands, he was able to conduct astronomical research that he could never have completed had his request for his own observatory in Groningen been granted.

includes training and preparation for conducting independent research and oc-
cupying social positions requiring scientific training.' In order to train their students as independent researchers, lecturers had to be accomplished researchers
themselves. Universities henceforth became research centres.

To adequately fulfil this new task, professors needed access to more extensive research facilities such as modern laboratories and a larger library with their
attendant personnel. In the years following the adoption of the new law, Groningen acquired a series of new university buildings that radically transformed
the city landscape: new structures were built for ophthalmology (1879), pharmacy
(1880), hygiene and bacteriology (1884), paediatrics (1891), physics (1892), bot-
any (1889), mineralogy and geology (1901), pathology (1903), anatomy (1909),
physiology (1911) and chemistry (1912). These buildings did not follow any form of
urban planning. They appeared in an ad-hoc manner whenever the need for a
new building became too urgent to further delay construction. Locations were
chosen because they were already owned by the university (e.g. in the immediate vicinity of the Academy Building and the Hortus Botanicus) or because they
happened to become available. This is why so many new laboratories were built

*32. Gerardus Heymans,
professor of philosophy
and psychology,
1890-1927.*

33. After the fire of the Academy Building in August 1906, students pose in the remains of the building.

on the location of the former fortification walls surrounding the old city centre. These sites were owned by the state, which sold some to the city (for housing or parks) while also keeping some for the construction of national buildings such as university laboratories. These buildings all looked alike and were designed by the same architects – the chief government architects of the Department of Education, Arts and Science Jacob van Lokhorst and his successor Jan Vrijman – who designed them in their favourite styles: neo-Gothic or neo-Renaissance.

The facilities listed so far were all built to serve scientific and medical disciplines. But the humanities were not entirely forgotten. Humanities experts repeatedly argued that what the laboratory was to the sciences, the library was to the humanities. It was therefore a crucial step for them when the University Library, still located behind the Catholic church in Broerstraat, was thoroughly extended and modernized in 1898. However, the most striking construction project by far was the complex of the new academic hospital on the former embankment on the eastern side of the city, the Oostersingel (1903). The complex included many separate clinics in the form of pavilions (for internal medicine, surgery, women's diseases and psychiatry) and a series of common buildings. Hidden from view, on the other hand, was the first psychology laboratory in the Netherlands, because in 1892 it was established at the private home of the professor of philosophy and psychology, Gerardus Heymans. This laboratory later relocated to the basement of the Academy Building – that is to say, in the *new* Academy Building because

34. *The official opening of the new Academy Building in June 1909. The opening act was performed by the Queen Wilhelmina's husband, Prince Hendrik, since the Queen had given birth to a daughter earlier that year and was unable to come.*

in August 1906, the classicist building that had been the heart of the university since 1850 burned to the ground, including the extensive natural history museum on the attic level with all of Camper's specimens. The only survivor was a mounted squirrel that happened to be at the home of the professor of zoology. To prevent any discussion of whether the University of Groningen should be closed down completely, given that it suffered such a great loss, plans were immediately made for reconstruction. Within a few days, the chief government architect Vrijman presented a design strongly reminiscent of one of his earlier designs (a gymnasium in The Hague) that perfectly matched the old building's intact foundations. This saved time and money. The new Academy Building was built in neo-Renaissance style, allegedly because this would have been the style chosen by the original university administrators if they had been at liberty to commission a new university building in 1614. In June 1909, Queen Wilhelmina's husband, Prince Hendrik, officially opened the building, which has since been the proud centre of Groningen university life. The Academy Building was the place where curators and senators met, where newly appointed professors held inaugural lectures, where the academic year was officially opened on the third Tuesday in September, where faculties held meetings, where lectures were given, and where many generations of students sat their candidate and doctoral examinations (and where some went on to defend their PhD theses).

Changes in the student world

After the Academy Building, the main centre of student life was Mutua Fides, the club building of Vindicat atque Polit, which was the fraternity that in theory all students were members of. Vindicat met in rented rooms (usually above a café) until well into the 19th century, but in 1883, for the first time, the fraternity acquired a building of its own, the new Mutua Fides on the northern side of the Grote Markt. This lavishly decorated building exuded power and pride and pro-

35. The Mutua Fides Society on the Grote Markt in Groningen, opened in 1883. It was here that the student fraternity Vindicat atque Polit gathered until the building was destroyed at the end of the Second World War.

63

vided sufficient space for a rich student life, replete with its own cultural, intellectual and sports associations (the student rowing association Aegir was founded in 1878). But there were also dark clouds on the horizon: despite Vindicat being open to all students, an increasing number of students refused to join and went on to found their own competing fraternities. This led to the establishment of a Catholic fraternity (Albertus Magnus) in 1896 and a Reformed fraternity (Veri et Recti Amici, VERA) in 1899. These fraternities were not very large at first, but they did break Vindicat's claimed monopoly on representing student interests. There were also students (known as the Nihilists) who did not join any fraternity because they found Vindicat too expensive or the atmosphere unpleasant. The rough hazing practices, which increasingly led to social criticism around 1900, were also a thorn in its side. None of this, however, made Vindicat feel particularly threatened.

A more serious threat was the surge in the number of female students from around 1900. In 1898, for the first time, a female student – probably Dody Kapteyn, daughter of the professor of astronomy – applied for membership of Vindicat. Following a heated discussion, her application was rejected. From this time onwards, Vindicat stipulated that it was only open to male students. Since they could not join Vindicat, a few female students decided to create their own sorority, Magna Pete (November 1898). Incidentally, relations between Vindicat and Magna Pete were very friendly from the start, with Magna Pete acting as the female counterpart of Vindicat.

In 1900, the presence of female students in Dutch universities was by no means commonplace. No objections had been voiced as long as female students were few and far between, but this changed when their number reached the dozens. (By 1910-1911, Groningen was home to 427 male and a total of 127 female students.) Female students tended to enrol in degree programmes in modern languages to obtain a secondary school teacher qualification, but disciplines such as pharmaceutical science and biology also attracted many female students. As the female student body grew in every Dutch university, so did resistance to them, for example from professors who believed that women were unsuited for academic studies. They claimed that women were too emotional and were more zealous than intelligent and thus unequipped for the hard discipline required by modern science. In Groningen, there was little such resistance, and the first female lecturer in the Netherlands, Marie Loke, was appointed lecturer in French without much dissent in 1907.

The most thorough Dutch refutation of the claim that women were unsuited for academia also happened to come from a Groningen professor, the previously mentioned Heymans. This philosopher, who accrued great fame in Germany for his psychic monism theory – in which he claimed that everything was conscious-

36. Female students during a lecture by the chemistry lecturer Hugo Rudolf Kruyt, 1910. Kruyt was filling in for the chemistry professor Frans Maurits Jaeger, who at the time was on a research leave in the United States.

ness – also introduced experimental methods to the field of psychology. When commissioned by a German colleague to write a treatise on women's psychology for a book series, Heymans launched a large-scale survey to collect data on the female psyche. He concluded that while the average woman might be slightly more emotional and industrious than the average man, the differences between men were greater than those between the sexes and, despite certain gradual differences in talent and character, women were as suited to academia as men. His book, *The Psychology of Women* (1910), was an important source of support for the feminists of the time.

Apotheosis

Like his friend Kapteyn, Heymans was one of the celebrities of the University of Groningen and of Dutch academia in general at the dawn of the 20th century. Around the turn of the century, Dutch scholars once again played an important international role, as illustrated by the relatively high number of Nobel Prizes awarded to Dutch researchers (if there had been Nobel Prize for Philosophy and Astronomy, they would undoubtedly have gone to Heymans and Kapteyn respec-

37. The Irish mathematician Alicia Boole Stott on her way from the New Church, where the 1914 honorary doctorates were awarded, to City Hall in the middle of the city.

tively). Among researchers, pride in their own achievements went hand in hand with a strong international orientation. Dutch intellectuals believed that, as a relatively small country with little international power, the Netherlands was ideally positioned to act as custodian of international law, more so than large powerful countries that were heavily invested in consolidating and expanding their own interests. The Netherlands, they argued, had no reason to fear that their call to act as a guardian of international law would be seen as a covert attempt to promote their own interests. They also viewed their country as an ideal mediator for large neighbouring nations such as France, England and Germany. This awareness of the Netherlands' exceptional task in the world formed the central idea behind the University of Groningen's celebrations on the occasion of its 300th anniversary in June 1914.

Never before had the university held a celebration on such a grand scale. Despite being more 'Dutch' than ever, the university was also thriving as never before, and it wished to advertise this fact. A bulky commemorative volume was published in which history professor Johan Huizinga masterfully described the university's history in the 19th century. In addition, honorary doctorates were awarded, processions were organized by students, and concerts were given: it was one big festival of national and international science. The internationally renowned physiologist and Rector Magnificus, Hartog Jacob Hamburger, who had hosted the 9th International Congress of Physiology in his new laboratory as recently as 1913, addressed his Dutch and international guests in French, German, English and Italian. He made a clear point that while researchers might be grounded in their national cultures, they also contributed to international science and research, and he sketched how science in particular had had a salutary effect on European civilization in the 19th century. Hamburger was aware of mounting tensions in Europe, but he skilfully navigated around them in his speech. The only sour note was that the rector of the University of Prague had to cut his stay in Groningen short because of rising tensions in Austria-Hungary in response to the assassination of Crown Prince Franz Ferdinand and his wife in Sarajevo. But after a few days, these tensions seemed to ebb away and Groningen was able to resume its basking in the aftermath of a magnificent anniversary celebration.

38. *Foreign guests at the 300th anniversary of the University of Groningen, 1914.*

4 /

39. *In 1939, mobi-
lized soldiers in uni-
form were allowed
to attend lectures.*

War and threats (1914-1945)

The First World War surprised everyone, including university administrators, and despite Dutch neutrality, it greatly affected daily life at the University of Groningen. The university went through a period of sobriety in which international contact came to a near complete standstill. Following the Treaty of Versailles, university life slowly blossomed once again, the borders opened, and adventurous professors took their students on excursions abroad. A period of modest growth followed, but by the 1930s, the university had to defend itself yet again against threats of extensive cutbacks and even partial closure. While immediate danger was averted, an awareness of the university's vulnerability remained. The University of Groningen was on the eve of some of the blackest pages in its history.

Cyclone of war violence

At the opening of the academic year in September 1914, Rector Magnificus Hamburger expressed his disbelief and confusion. Barely a month after the university's festive lustrum celebration ('that brotherly gathering of sons from the most diverse of nations'), a 'cyclone of war violence' had begun raging over Europe, and hostility and hate reigned supreme. The First World War was a fact. Although the Netherlands adopted a neutral stance and was able to avoid going to war, daily life was still severely affected, including university life. Many senior students and some lecturers were mobilized in the summer of 1914 and sent to guard the borders, resulting in a drop in student numbers from more than 600 in 1913-1914 to 470 in 1914-1915. These were sober years, with no room for festivities, serenading or student frivolities.

Academic work continued, albeit in a reduced form, with the exception of international academic contacts, which more or less came to a halt as travelling had become impossible. This directly affected the astronomer Kapteyn who was

40. *The Timbertown Follies: a cabaret company by British soldiers in the Groningen 'English Camp'.*

conducting research in the US when the war broke out. He wanted to return to Groningen immediately, but German sea mines made navigation between the US and Europe impossible for a long time, and he was only able to make the crossing nearly six months later.

Until 1917, the war felt quite far away from Groningen. There were, of course, Belgian refugees requiring asylum, and after the fall of Antwerp (October 1914), 1,500 British troops escaped to the Netherlands and remained interned in Groningen until the end of the war in what was called the 'English Camp'. As the war progressed, these British soldiers and officers were increasingly granted more freedom, and they took part in cultural life by giving cabaret performances and offering boxing and rowing lessons for students. During the last year of the war, the situation worsened. Food became scarce and fuel was rationed. Some research projects came to a standstill because of a lack of gas or coal, and students could no longer heat or light their rooms. The severe winter led to Spartan working conditions. Luckily, the university was able to open a few heated rooms in the Academy Building, a service the students made grateful use of.

Overall, the University of Groningen came out of the war unharmed and even with a certain sense of optimism. Student numbers rose to new heights, which allowed for new academic staff to be hired. The university was growing once again.

International fraternization

International collaboration slowly resumed in the post-war years. Just after the war, Groningen professors were still forced to turn down invitations to lustrum celebrations of foreign universities because the preparation time was too short or the distance unbridgeable (e.g. to the University of Dunedin in New Zealand), but from the early 1920s onwards, international contacts grew once again. Groningen professors attended conferences, gave lectures at foreign universities, and joined anniversary celebrations. International celebrities came to Groningen for guest lectures, culminating in the annual Aula Lecture. The Faculty of Medicine organized student exchanges with the universities of Leuven and Ghent. Enterprising professors such as the popular chemist Hilmar Backer and Groningen's first female professor, the geneticist Jantina Tammes, took their students on excursions to Hamburg, Berlin, Paris, Rome and London. These were mostly individual contacts and personal initiatives, and there was no international policy as such, but after a period of isolation, wanderlust was once again on the rise. The rector's annual account of university life for these years includes long lists of travelling professors and student excursions.

Renewed contact with Germany and Austria, the Central European nations that had lost the war, was still a sensitive matter. In the years immediately follow-

41. Groningen's first female professor Jantina Tammes on a student excursion in Berlin (1931).

42. 'The triumph of science', mural by the German brothers Otto and Rudolf Linnemann in the auditorium of the Academy Building (1914-1954).

ing the war, a fierce debate was waged in Europe concerning collaboration with German and Austrian researchers. France and Belgium were categorically against it. They blamed their German colleagues in particular for blindly contributing to the war effort and advocated establishing an entirely new International Research Council (IRC) without the Central European nations. Dutch scholars were divided about joining the IRC. Most professors were oriented towards Germany, and because of the Netherlands' neutrality during the war, there was no strong anti-German sentiment in the Netherlands. Prominent Groningen professors such as Kapteyn, Heymans and Hamburger were even strongly opposed to excluding Central European researchers and pleaded for international fraternization. They gave up in disappointment when the national Royal Academy of Arts and Sciences joined the IRC. It was not until 1925 that German scholars were cautiously granted access to this international organization.

In Groningen, fraternization with Germany and Austria was already taking shape in the years immediately following the war. In the spring of 1919, the German theologian Ernst Troelsch was invited to give a lecture at the Groningen theological faculty association, and later that year a Groningen representative attended the 500th anniversary of the University of Rostock. Groningen student organizations united to collect money and clothing for the much-impoverished German and Austrian students. On the invitation of the Magna Pete sorority, 40 Viennese students visited Groningen for a few weeks in the summer of 1920 to recharge their mental batteries. They were housed in the former English Camp. With a festive evening and a varied excursion programme, Groningen students demonstrated their international solidarity.

Father of excursions

Professor Hilmar Johannes Backer (1882-1959) was a modest and unobtrusive man, but he made a lasting impression on his students. His excursions in the Netherlands and abroad were particularly legendary. While on excursion in Hamburg with 40 students, he stopped a passing empty city bus and managed, with a 'Zum Bahnhof', to convince the driver to take him and his group to the station so they would not miss their train. Nor was he deterred by the closed doors of the British Museum of Natural History in London. He simply rang the doorbell and spoke so convincingly and at such length to the astounded museum employee that the poor man had no choice but to allow Backer and his students into the museum, albeit under light protest: 'This is quite an exception, sir.'

Backer was appointed professor of organic chemistry in Groningen in 1916. He remained a bachelor his whole life and saw his students and staff as his 'organic family'. He thought students should experience more than textbooks and lecture halls and therefore organized excursions to chemical factories in the Netherlands and, after the First World War, also to other countries. In 1920, he took 20 chemistry students and a geologist to Hannover and the Harz to visit a salt mine, an ore mine and a number of factories. A year later, he organized a successful 14-day excursion to Bohemia in which students from Utrecht and Amsterdam as well as a number of his colleagues took part. Money was no problem; the excursions were very affordable, and Backer created a support fund for less wealthy students. Participants reported enthusiastically on these fantastic trips that included cultural excursions and meetings with international students and professors. Lovingly, they described Backer as a 'caring and thoughtful leader' and a 'true father of excursions'.

43. Hilmar Backer with students at a fruit stall in front of the National Gallery in London (1925).

44. *A group of international archaeologists visits the excavation of renowned senior lecturer and future professor of archeology Albert Egges van Giffen in Ezinge, a village 15 km northwest of the city of Groningen (1932).*

Impending shrinkage

The idealism and international solidarity of Groningen students was characteristic of the new zeitgeist. Old pre-war relations were disintegrating. The Netherlands had become a full-fledged democracy with the introduction of general suffrage for all Dutch men and women in 1917 and 1919, respectively. At the University of Groningen, relationships were also shifting. The introduction of a scholarship system for the 'impecunious' opened the university's doors to new groups of students. Over the course of a decade, the number of students and academic staff doubled, and in 1924 Groningen celebrated the enrolment of 1,000 students.

Professors had to get used to the presence of students from different social backgrounds and wondered out loud whether society needed so many academics. They feared the development of 'an academic proletariat'. This fear was subsequently often voiced at times of economic recession, high unemployment and budget cuts. It was symptomatic of the gradual but unavoidable shift from a system of elitist universities to higher education for all.

In the 1930s, the worldwide economic crisis hit the university with a series of cutbacks. In 1934, a new law was passed that made it nearly impossible for students from abroad to study in the Netherlands, to the consternation of the Groningen rector, who believed this cutback would impair the international character of academic research. In 1935, when it became apparent that general budget cuts would not be sufficient, a ghost from the past made its appearance: the idea of closing down or at least seriously truncating one of the universities emerged once again, with Groningen as the main target. A strong lobby group was immediately initiated by the Groningen community. The municipality and the province took it upon themselves to bear a larger portion of the running costs of the academic hospital in an attempt to deflect the impending cutbacks. Once again, the anchoring of the University of Groningen in the city and region turned out to be its salvation. Thanks to this pressure and the diplomacy of the curators, a truncation of the university was avoided. As early as 1935, retiring Rector Magnificus Gerardus van der Leeuw was able to announce that the university would be saved. However, he spoke out strongly against a national government which he said viewed the north of the country as a kind of 'colony' and continuously threatened and marginalized Groningen compared to universities in the west of the country.

The rector was even more vocal in deploring the growing trend towards seeing universities as professional training schools. He believed that the university's power lay in weaving together teaching and research. Only by doing so could universities continue to fulfil their traditional role as an organ of civilization and moral compass, something the rector felt was direly needed in the bleak years of the 1930s.

Refugees from the east

Traditionally, the University of Groningen had tried as much as possible to keep politics outside its walls. But when Hitler and the National Socialists came to power in Germany in 1933 and the first news of the dismissal of Jewish professors reached the Netherlands, this position could no longer be maintained. The Groningen rector immediately called on other universities to jointly protest against this injustice, but he only received support from his colleagues in Utrecht and Nijmegen. The university's contacts with German scholars remained intact. Various German guest speakers visited Groningen in the 1930s and some return visits were made, but official invitations from Germany were subject to critical scrutiny. For example, the Groningen sports physiologist Frederik Buytendijk refused to give a lecture at an international conference on the occasion of the Olympic Games in Berlin (1936), and the Jewish Rector Magnificus Leonard Polak Daniëls refused, on

45. The Jewish-German philosopher Helmuth Plessner fled Germany and came to Groningen in 1934. He was the first professor of sociology at the Groningen university (1939-1943) and later professor of philosophy (1946-1951). Portrait by Paul Citroen (1951).

principle, to attend the 550th anniversary of the University of Heidelberg. He took a clear political stance and denounced the German exclusion of Jewish scholars.

The university senate was cautious in its response to incoming students and refugees from the East. As early as in the summer of 1933, many German and Eastern European students applied for a degree programme in Groningen, 35 to the Faculty of Medicine alone. The senate members were divided in their response, and most applicants were turned down in anticipation of the 1934 law that would put a break on international student enrolment. A few Jewish scholars were warmly welcomed. At Buytendijk's invitation, the Cologne philosopher Helmuth Plessner came to Groningen, first as a guest lecturer, but thanks to the financial support of the American Rockefeller Foundation he was able to obtain a permanent position. Plessner would have preferred to go to England or the US but ended up staying on in Groningen as lecturer in philosophical anthropology and professor by special appointment in sociology (and after the war as full professor of philosophy until 1951). From Groningen, he forged a strong connection with the University of Göttingen in the 1960s.

In the general student magazine, *Der Clercke Cronike*, vigorous debates arose in the 1930s concerning the danger of the rise of fascism and National Socialism. As early as 1932, Leo Frank, a law and philosophy student, published a series of seven articles analyzing in great detail the danger of the developments taking place in Germany and Italy. He was also one of the first to foresee the impending exclusion of Jewish scholars. The ensuing debate showed that many students underestimated or even trivialized the political threat of the emerging National Socialist movement. They did not believe things could or would deteriorate so quickly.

Dark chapter

On 1 September 1939, Germany invaded Poland and Europe was at war. The Dutch army was already on the alert, and approximately one-third of the male students and a number of staff members were called to arms. On 10 May 1940, the Germans invaded the Netherlands, and after a short struggle a five-year period of occupation began.

The University of Groningen lived through one of the darkest chapters of its history. Immediately after the capitulation, former Rector Magnificus Polak Daniëls committed suicide and another Jewish professor, the philosopher Leo Polak, tried in vain to flee to England with his family. University administrators mostly called on everyone to remain calm, an attitude they maintained through-

46. The German-Swiss theologian Karl Barth delivers a lecture for Groningen students of theology (1939).

out the war and one that was definitely driven by a wish to protect the university that had so frequently been threatened. Yet there was also a positive note in the summer of 1940: in a monastery near the Groningen village of Ter Apel, a group of 200 students, professors, and administrators met for a five-day summer course that powerfully asserted the close ties within the academic community. For a long time afterwards, people spoke with nostalgia of 'the spirit of Ter Apel'.

These ties were soon put under pressure as a result of the measures imposed by the German occupiers. After the summer, and to the great dissatisfaction of Groningen professors, Johannes Marie Neele Kapteyn, the *deutschfreundliche* professor of Old Germanic, was appointed rector instead of their first choice, the liberal Combertus Willem van der Pot. Two years later, Kapteyn was replaced by the anatomist Herman Maximilien de Burlet, an outspoken National Socialist. This allowed the Germans to tighten their control over the university.

In the autumn of 1940, Jewish lecturers and staff members were suspended and a few months later dismissed. The philosopher Leo Polak protested against his exclusion and was promptly arrested and sent to the Sachsenhausen concen-

47. *The Jewish professor of philosophy Leo Polak was arrested by the Germans in February 1941 for challenging his dismissal. Later that year he was deported to the Sachsenhausen concentration camp and murdered. Portrait by Otto Boudewijn de Kat (1973).*

48. Disbandment meeting of the student organization VERA in the second year of the war. Students sing the Dutch national anthem (31 October 1941).

tration camp where he died in late 1941. The next step undertaken by the National Socialists was to exclude Jewish students from the university. In response to these measures, students threatened to strike, but after being pressured by the university administrators, they limited themselves to writing a letter of protest. In late 1941, the student magazine was banned under German censorship and Jews were barred from fraternities. This was the last straw, and nearly all fraternities discontinued their activities.

Teaching did continue until 1943, when the Germans demanded that all students sign a declaration of loyalty stating that they would not resist the occupiers. This turned into a fiasco for the Germans. Only 10% of the students signed at first, leading to the announcement of the next measure: anyone who refused to sign was to report for labour duty in Germany. This marked a deathblow to student resistance. Some students signed the declaration, a few hundred reported for labour duty and many went into hiding. The university officially remained open, but academic life in actuality ground to a halt. Only the academic hospital remained open.

The University of Groningen thus emerged from the war unharmed but battered. While the universities of Leiden and Delft were closed by the Germans in response to protests against the exclusion of Jewish staff members, Groningen

Anda Kerkhoven

At the age of 19, medical student Anda Kerkhoven (1919-1945), exchanged the tropical island of Java for cold Groningen, where she obtained an exemption from dissection practicals. Kerkhoven was a fierce opponent of vivisection, a vegan and a radical pacifist who was seen by her fellow students as somewhat unworldly. During the German occupation, she remained faithful to her principles and actively took part in a non-violent resistance group until her arrest in December 1944. On the morning of 19 March 1945, barely a month before the liberation of Groningen, she was executed on an abandoned dirt road. Anda Kerkhoven is immortalized on a stained-glass winow in the Aula of the Academy Building together with another idealist: Aletta Jacobs, the Netherlands' first female student.

49. *Anda Kerkhoven (right) and Aletta Jacobs (left) on a stained glass window in the university auditorium, by Johan Dijkstra (1951).*

remained open like most other Dutch universities. But Groningen had been very compliant indeed with its pro-German rectors and administrators who were forever apprehensive of a forced and perhaps permanent closure. This was also the opinion of its students after the war, who demanded a substantial purge not only of pro-German administrators and professors but also of the students who had signed the German declaration of loyalty. Once again, a conflict arose between the students and the administrators. The sanctions imposed on those who had signed the declaration (exclusion from lectures for a period of a few months to a year and a half) were considered by many to be too mild. These students held on to their ideal of the university as a moral community, while many of those who had signed took a more pragmatic approach. The faith in a strong and united university community had been dealt a tremendous blow.

5/

50. *Opening of the academic year 1945; on the left, the ruins of the building of the Vindicat student association.*

Growing pains and democratization (1945-1980)

After the war, the University of Groningen quickly reopened its doors so that students could resume their studies. After a period of total isolation, the need for international contact was so great that the unbridled wanderlust of some professors caused a number of rectors to express their concern. It soon became clear that the close-knit, small-scale, pre-war academic community was a thing of the past. The university grew – gradually at first, but starting from the late 1950s at a surprisingly fast pace. The almighty professors were taken down from their pedestals by emancipated students who demanded full participation. The University of Groningen took a unique stance in this process of democratization.

The renewal of the university

On 16 April 1945, Canadian troops evicted the German occupiers from Groningen, and on 5 May all of the Netherlands was free after a long struggle and a hard winter of hunger. Groningen was one of the first universities in the Netherlands to reopen its doors. This was no problem, because the university buildings were largely unscathed. Rector Magnificus Van der Pot, appointed at last after having been passed over in 1940 in favour of the pro-German Kapteyn, immediately called on students to resume their studies and in this way contribute to the country's restoration. As early as June, the first students reported for 'duty', and within a few months their number reached a record and the lecture halls were filled to capacity. Soon the call for purges had died down.

Should universities carry on as they had before the war? In a brochure entitled *De vernieuwing der universiteit* (1945) (*The Renewal of the University*), six professors, led by the professor of comparative religion Van der Leeuw and by Rector Magnificus Van der Pot, argued that they shouldn't. Students had shown themselves to be resilient under the occupation, but the lack of moral responsibility

51. *Gerardus van der Leeuw (1890-1950) was an influential theologian and historian of religion. In 1933, he published his most important work* Phänomenologie der Religion *in German, translated in English as* Religion in Essence and Manifestation: A Study in Phenomenology. *From 1945-1946, Van der Leeuw was Minister of Education for the Labour Party. Portrait by Annemarie Busschers (2014).*

among the staff was strongly criticized: 'most saw themselves more as administrators in a difficult situation than as spiritual leaders and responsible educators of the youth.' The professors felt that the universities had hidden for too long behind their position of neutrality. They called on the new university to represent clear spiritual values grounded in Christian humanism. A radical renewal of academic education was needed, with more attention given to the relationship between disciplines and general training for students instead of a school-like approach purely focused on training in specific subjects. The professors dreamt of helping students grow into spiritual and social leaders with their own individual perspectives. When Van der Leeuw was appointed Minister of Education in 1945, he established a national committee that advised all universities to organize *Studium Generale* programmes: general lectures to help all students develop a broad perspective on science and society. Groningen was one of the first to organize a *Studium Generale*, in September 1946, which at first only drew a small number of students. It was not until the 1960s, however, that the *Studium Generale* became a successful counterweight to the compartmentalization of higher education and for the programmes to become open to ordinary citizens and act as a bridge to society.

University renewal was less swift than the authors of the brochure had hoped. Their ideal of a close-knit academic community in particular turned out to be incompatible with a fast-growing university. On the eve of the war, Groningen had 859 regular students, and by 1945-1946 this had increased to 1,474, only to pass 2,000 a few years later: a twofold increase in ten years. The need for a university degree was great after years in which education had more or less come to a standstill. In addition, many new professors saw the university primarily as an institution that should train experts and in this way make its contribution to the restoration. Attempts to revive 'the spirit of Ter Apel' and the community spirit of the first year of the war with an annual summer course seemed to succeed at first. In 1946, approximately 140 students and 20 lecturers took part in a five-day gathering in Ter Apel. A year later, their number had shrunk by half, and the year after that there were so few applications that the gathering was cancelled. Clearly, the close-knit pre-war university community was a thing of the past.

Open to the world

Perhaps one of the key developments in the post-war era was the growing need for international contacts. Immediately after the liberation, material help was mobi-

52. *Summer course in Ter Apel, July 1940. Standing behind the students are chemist Hilmar Backer and historian Pieter Jan van Winter (with pipe). After the war, there was a short revival of the summer courses.*

lized from abroad, with food parcels arriving from Denmark and textbooks from the Swiss University of Neuchâtel, which had adopted Groningen. High-ranking Canadian military officers gave guest lectures about their country's culture, and a stream of international guest speakers made their appearance. After a period of isolation, professors and students felt more than ever the need for international contacts. Students eagerly seized opportunities to study abroad. In the spring of 1946, for example, a group of 23 students accepted an invitation from the University of Neuchâtel to study for a few months in Switzerland. Other countries, such as England and Czechoslovakia, offered individual grants that students made grateful use of.

An important role was played by the Groningen International Student Service (ISS), an ideological organization that promoted European student exchange. Via ISS, students who had been active in the resistance movement could take part in a study trip through Russia, and students who had suffered physical or psychological injury during the war were offered a study trip to England complete with nursing care. After the war, the doors to the world were suddenly thrown wide open, and students showed more interest in international politics than they had done in the pre-war years. Indonesia's struggle for independence was openly discussed, as was the correct attitude the Dutch should take towards their former German occupier.

Eastern Europe was a popular destination at first, until the communist coup in Czechoslovakia. In response, the university broke off official relations with universities in the Eastern Bloc, although guest and refugee students from communist countries continued to be warmly welcomed. With the support of the University Asylum Fund, two Czechoslovakian students studied in Groningen, and after the Hungarian Revolution of 1956 was violently put down by the Soviet Army, the university offered a safe place to 12 Hungarian students.

Unlike in pre-war years, when contacts had been established mostly on an individual level, the academic community increasingly developed ongoing relationships with foreign universities. Via cultural agreements established by the Minister of Education, Van der Leeuw, funds became available for structural exchange programmes with countries such as Belgium, France and England. The University of Groningen entered into a long-term relationship with the University of Newcastle. Groningen professors travelled around the globe attending conferences, giving lectures and acting as guest lecturers. In the early 1950s, many rectors lamented in their annual addresses that the professors' insatiable wanderlust took a heavy toll on work at their home university.

Each year, 80 to 90 professors and staff members travelled abroad for study trips, conferences, guest lectures, meetings with colleagues and research. These trips were usually born out of individual contacts with colleagues in other indus-

A student as a birthday gift

T he University of Groningen's collaboration with the Georg-August-Univer-
sität in Göttingen was largely the work of an old acquaintance: sociologist
Helmuth Plessner, who had been appointed rector in Göttingen in 1960.
He contacted his Groningen colleague and counterpart, the sociologist Pieter
Jan Bouman, which led to a long-term relationship between the two universities.
Every year, delegations exchanged experiences, alternately in Groningen and in
Göttingen. On the occasion of its 350th anniversary, the University of Groningen
received a birthday gift from its German partner: a student was invited to study in
Göttingen for one year on a full grant. Folkert Postma, a Frisian farmer's son and
candidate student in history, was the lucky recipient of this gift and left for Göttin-
gen in September 1965.

On his return, Postma reported to the university senate. He praised the way in
which the University of Göttingen welcomed and supported international students
(whose number he estimated at around 750). A separate secretariat, the Auslands-
amt, was responsible for organizing everything from housing and excursions to
weekly dances aimed to encourage contact with German students. There was an
international student house where international students could choose between a
single room and a room shared with a German student. Daily meals were served. In
other words, international students were extremely well taken care of.

Not wishing to lag behind, the Groningen senate invited a German student to
study in Groningen for a year. This led to some discomfort among the officials responsible. Groningen did not have a secretariat for international student support,
and housing was an issue. In the end, the Head of the General Affairs Department reported to the senate that a solution had been found. The student could
be housed in a student flat as of 1 September 1967. However, he reported, 'as far
as support is concerned, matters are a little more complicated since we do not
have an "Auslandsreferent" as they do in Göttingen.' Perhaps the student coun-
sellors could help? The University of Groningen was clearly not yet professionally
equipped to receive and support international students.

trialized countries. Groningen also had permanent official exchange programmes with the universities of Newcastle, Strasbourg and Göttingen. Student mobility was still quite limited: a few dozen students of non-Dutch origin came to Groningen every year, mostly from the former Dutch colony of Indonesia. Until the mid-1960s, a surprisingly high number of Norwegian medical students came to the Netherlands because Norwegian programmes in medicine were subject to a maximum number of students.

Inspiration from America

A popular travel destination for professors and students was the US. During the war, the US had taken the scientific and technological lead and pursued an active cultural politics in which academic exchange played an important role. The post-war Fulbright grant programme allowed professors and students from the late 1940s to become acquainted with American academic life.

Traditionally, Dutch universities had been based on the German organizational model. Powerful professors reigned over their own little kingdoms and closely guarded the interests of their discipline. They were responsible for teaching and research and kept a suitable distance from their students. The university was a closed bastion where students were trained as academic scholars, without much attention paid to their future role in society. This hierarchical and closed system proved untenable after the war due to the growing university community and the greater openess to society. Dutch scholars began to observe the model of the US university with great interest.

In 1950, sociology professor Pieter Jan Bouman visited the US as a guest lecturer on a Fulbright grant. Before beginning his work at Ann Arbor, he travelled through the country on a Greyhound bus, an experience that opened his eyes. On his return, he wrote the essayistic booklet *Volk in beweging. Het onbegrepen Amerika* (*A People on the Move. The Misunderstood America*) in which he tried to refute the myth of American culture as boastful and superficial. He criticized the attitude of cultural superiority adopted by European universities and praised the teamwork, interdisciplinary collaboration and social engagement of American scholars. His booklet was much read but failed to convince everyone. For example, Groningen Rector Magnificus Marius Jacob Sirks openly deplored the 'Americanization' of Europe and the US tendency towards applied science and university marketing. At the opening of the academic year 1951-1952, he warned against the 'garish Harlequin suit of some American universities'.

Bouman was very much in touch with the zeitgeist, for the classic university system dominated by the professors gradually disintegrated and made way for a

53. *Professor of sociology Pieter Jan Bouman visited the US as a guest lecturer. He was impressed by the teamwork, interdisciplinary collaboration and social engagement of American scholars. Portrait by Erasmus Herman van Dulmen Kumpelman (1988).*

more egalitarian system. The sciences were the first to embrace this shift, and in Groningen, it was chemists who took the lead. As early as 1950, they welcomed an American guest lecturer who came to lectures wearing flamboyant shirts and asked his students to call him 'Bob'. This was a preview of the model embraced by Groningen chemists, which prioritized teamwork, the strive for excellence and international collaboration. Starting in the early 1960s, professors Hans Wijnberg and Jan Kommandeur, who had spent time in the US and Canada, championed this 'Groningen model'. They introduced small research teams with a stringent selection process and many temporary appointments; only top researchers were offered permanent positions. In addition, collaboration with other scientific disciplines and with industry was increasingly sought. This new approach was a great success. Within ten years, Groningen chemists had become world leaders in their field.

Explosive growth

In the first half of the 20th century, the university had grown very slowly: from 1,000 students in 1924 to 2,000 in 1950. But from the late 1950s onwards, the

The Real Inglorious Bastard

Hans Wijnberg (1922-2011) was a decisive and inspiring chemist who made an indelible mark on Groningen university life. Born into a Jewish family, he left for New York in 1939 with his twin brother, urged by their father. Hans studied at the Brooklyn Technical University and acquired US citizenship. During his military service he trained first as a parachutist and then as a secret agent. In February 1945, he took part in a secret mission. Together with two other spies, he was dropped from a plane in the Austrian Alps. The trio made their way through waist-deep snow towards Innsbruck and sent information about German troop deployment and military industry to the Allied headquarters in Italy. Their spectacular mission, which Wijnberg rarely spoke of, formed the inspiration for the film *Inglourious Basterds* by the American director Quentin Tarantino, who gave the story his own twist. Wijnberg remained in the US for a number of years after the war. His parents and younger brother had been killed in Auschwitz. Partly because of his war experiences, he always remained a staunch anti-fascist and anti-communist.

After the war, Wijnberg studied chemistry at Cornell University, defended his PhD there and worked as a researcher at various American universities. He only returned to the Netherlands in 1959, as a Fulbright professor in Leiden. A year later, he was appointed professor and director of the Organic Chemistry Laboratory in Groningen. An inspiring teacher, he led his research group with a firm hand and trained a number of top researchers, including Nobel Prize laureate Ben Feringa.

Wijnberg told the true story of his 1945 secret mission in the Canadian documentary *The Real Inglorious Bastards* (2012). The day after he gave his final interview for the documentary, he passed away.

growth rate accelerated, reaching 10,000 students in 1970. With a fivefold increase in barely 20 years, Groningen became the fastest growing university in the Netherlands, something no one had anticipated. Back in 1953, Rector Magnificus Jacob Houdijn Beekhuis had warned in his annual address of an impending decline in student numbers. Some faculties had seen their enrolment numbers halved. He blamed this national trend on people's reduced wealth. Economic recovery following the war was slow, and the children of less wealthy parents were unable to study due to a lack of funds. The rector foresaw a gloomy future.

Luckily, the university was given a welcome boost a few months later. On 4 November 1953, just before the curtain opened for an opera at the Stadsschouwburg (City Theater) in Groningen, Rector Magnificus Pieter Jan van Winter announced to the audience that Frits Zernike, professor of mathematical and technical physics, had won the Nobel Prize in Physics for his phase contrast microscope. Groningen could finally boast of having won a Nobel Prize. A few years later, the university narrowly missed a second opportunity to win this high distinction. Shortly after the war, the American chemist Willard Frank Libby had developed the carbon-14 dating method. Groningen physicist Hessel de Vries refined Libby's carbon-14 method into a reliable technique for archaeological

55. Groningen physicist Hessel de Vries (right) and the American chemist Willard Frank Libby (left), winner of the 1960 Nobel Prize in Chemistry for the development of the carbon-14 dating method.

91

First Nobel Prize – Phase contrast microscope

Groningen's first Nobel Prize laureate, Frits Zernike (1888-1966), studied chemistry in Amsterdam before becoming the assistant to the astronomer Jacobus Cornelius Kapteyn in Groningen in 1913. He trained as a chemist but gradually shifted to mathematical and technical physics and optics. After defending his dissertation in Amsterdam in 1915, he was appointed lecturer in theoretical physics in Groningen and was promoted to professor seven years later. In 1953, Zernike was awarded the Nobel Prize in Physics for his phase contrast microscope, a device that allowed researchers to map living cells without using contrast fluid.

The German optical factory Carl Zeiss originally showed no interest in Zernike's invention, but during the Second World War, they took the microscope into production without informing him. This microscope allowed breakthroughs in medicine and biology, and Zernike received the recognition he deserved after the war. It goes without saying that the University of Groningen was delighted with this first Nobel Prize, but the news was not broadly publicized. Zernike was modest and shy and avoided publicity as much as possible. On the day after the announcement, he went to work as if nothing had happened.

56. Nobel Prize laureate Frits Zernike and the phase contrast microscope.

57. The first university buildings in Paddepoel, on the northern outskirts of the city, later to become the Zernike Complex.

research. This could well have earned him a Nobel Prize were it not for the fact that he fell in love with his secretary. When she turned him down, he could not cope with being rejected and things escalated into a tragedy. In 1959, De Vries killed his beloved before taking his own life. A year later, Libby was awarded the Nobel Prize for his carbon-14 research.

By the late 1950s, the dark clouds anticipated by Rector Magnificus Beekhuis had dissipated. The Dutch economy was booming, and prosperity soared. A much more generous grant system was introduced, which resulted in student numbers increasing from 3,000 in 1959 to nearly 5,000 in 1961. In addition, the post-war baby boom led to the birth of an entirely new generation of students, the baby boomers, who took the universities by storm from 1963 onwards. In Groningen, the medical and science programmes grew fast, while the new faculties of economic and social sciences also attracted many students. At long last, funds became available to hire more staff. By 1964, the university had 1,700 full-time positions: 200 professors and lecturers, 700 research staff members and an administrative and support staff of 800. This sudden and unexpected expansion of scale required a commensurate spatial expansion.

By the late 1950s, the university had to concede that some of its buildings and laboratories had become outdated. In 1958, an extensive construction plan was created to concentrate university buildings into three clusters. Since its foundation in 1614, the university had been located in the city centre around the Academy Building on Broerstraat. In the new plan, the city centre remained the university's home base, with space for most faculties in a wide circle around the Academy Building. Following failed attempts to move the academic hospital to the outskirts of the city, it was finally decided that the Faculty of Medicine would remain on the hospital terrain at the edge of the city centre (the second cluster) where it had enough room to expand further.

An entirely new location was created at Paddepoel, a meadow area on the northern outskirts of the city. It offered enough space to meet the needs of the science faculty. After some delays and the inevitable hurdles, the plan for the third cluster was given shape and new science buildings appeared at Paddepoel in the second half of the 1960s. The biologists did not relocate to Paddepoel but moved instead to the southern village of Haren because the soil there was more suitable for a Hortus Botanicus. Paddepoel, later renamed the Zernike Complex, grew into an external campus accommodating not only the natural sciences but also economics, business administration, and the spatial sciences. It also included the Center for Advanced Radiation Technology and the University Sports Centre, with the later addition of a business park – the Zernike Science Park. With the 1993 addition of large sections of the Hanze University of Applied Sciences (a fusion of all Groningen applied sciences programmes), Zernike grew into the largest concentration of higher education in Groningen.

Silent revolution

Coinciding with the university's rapid growth and expansion in scale, a silent revolution was taking place: computerization. This development was to revolutionize university research, teaching and organization over the next 50 years, and it ultimately may have been what saved universities. Without the automation of various university administrative tasks, the explosive growth in student and staff numbers might well have become unmanageable. In the Netherlands, the University of Groningen led the way in this rapid progression from simple computing machines to number-crunching supercomputers.

In the 1950s, chemists, astronomers and mathematicians were the first to feel the need for greater computing power. The chemist Donald Smits was asked to investigate what computing machine (the term 'computer' was not yet used) was most suitable for the university. The choice fell on the ZEBRA (*Zeer Eenvoudige Binaire Rekenautomaat*, Very Simple Binary Computing Machine), a device with a speed of 500 computations per second and an internal memory of 32 kb that came into use in 1959. The ZEBRA served the entire university and was so large

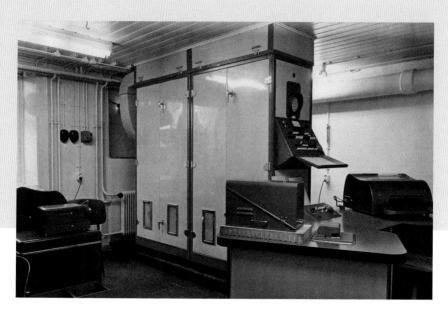

58. *ZEBRA, the first university computing machine.*

that it filled an entire cellar room in the recently opened Mathematics Institute. It was able to operate 24 hours a day due to the efforts of working students. Its use was reserved for a select group of researchers; students were only allowed access under exceptional circumstances and at a fee.

Five years later, the ZEBRA had already been replaced by Telefunken's TR4, a device that was 100 times faster. The TR4 was given its own building, the *Reken-centrum* (Computation Centre), with Donald Smits as its first director. The TR4 was used not only for the natural sciences but also by psychologists, sociologists and medical experts to process survey and statistical data. Generations of central computers followed one after the other at a rapid pace. Groningen and Amsterdam led the way with their purchases of supercomputers from the Cyber series, with a power of 5 million computations per second. The media loved it and printed headlines such as 'Computing machine: 4,800,000 times faster than a pencil.' It was only with the advent of personal computers in the mid-1980s that the new technology became accessible to all students and staff.

New relationships

The expansion in scale did more than open university doors to new groups of students, it also changed the role of professors. Until the Second World War, nearly all professors had lived in the city of Groningen. They worked from home, invited students for tea and administered examinations from home. This changed after the war, as professors increasingly moved out of the city, and by the 1960s, examinations at a professor's home had become rare. Relationships among students also changed. Students no longer came primarily from the elite classes but also from the middle and even working classes. They brought with them their own perspectives on academic life and were less committed to traditional etiquette and mores. The 'working student' had been a largely unheard-of phenomenon in pre-war years, but by the 1960s, 40% of students had a job on the side. The classic suit-wearing student was now confronted with pipe-smoking activists in jeans turning their noses up at elitist fraternities. Traditional fraternities lost ground, and before long, Vindicat's hegemony could no longer be taken for granted.

Following the establishment of a student parliament with public elections for all students in 1964, Vindicat lost to the left-wing *Studentenvakbeweging* (SVB, Student Labour Union), a national democratization movement that advocated more say for students and student pay. And so it was that SVB member Jacques Wallage was elected president of the student parliament and appeared in his official role at academic ceremonies, thus usurping the role traditionally held by the rector of Vindicat. Vindicat's monopoly was broken.

As a sociology student, Wallage and the SVB had a clear objective: they wanted to break open the closed academic world: 'We believed that isolated student life, with its sports facilities and infrastructure, would soon disappear. Students would become regular city residents. We were also convinced that Vindicat would disband within a decade. That was a miscalculation.' Wallage went on to become a prominent politician. After his graduation, he was elected council member and alderman for the *Partij van de Arbeid* (the Dutch Labour Party) and pursued a successful career in national politics before returning to Groningen as mayor.

Vindicat was able to recover from the revolutionary 1960s. In an attempt to accommodate the new zeitgeist, it discontinued its controversial hazing practices, if only temporarily. It also fused with its female counterpart, Magna Pete, and opened its doors to students from the University of Applied Sciences. But the days of its hegemony were over: from this point onwards, Vindicat became simply one of the many Groningen fraternities.

Democratic governance

The expanding university required sound management. A new law passed in 1960 (the *Wet Wetenschappelijk Onderwijs*, WWO) granted the universities more autonomy, with operational management no longer the responsibility of the Minister of Education but of local university administrators. The former dual system in which professors and the rector (the senate) had decided on matters concerning teaching and research and a select group of administrators (the curators) were responsible for operational management had become obsolete. Also, students were demanding a more active role. After years of entreaties and negotiations, this resulted in an administrative model unique to Groningen – the *Tussentijdse Bestuursvorm* (TBV, interim governance model) – in which curators, researchers, technical and administrative personnel and students jointly governed the university. In particular, the full-fledged position of students in the university's day-to-day management was unique in the Netherlands.

This experimental governance model only lasted one year (from 1971 to 1972). In the meantime, the Dutch House of Representatives had adopted the *Wet Universitaire Bestuurshervorming* (University Governance Reform Act), which was also implemented in Groningen. The curators and the senate disappeared from the stage. From 1972 onwards, day-to-day management was entrusted to a professional university board that included the rector but no students. A democratically elected university council of students and staff acted as a kind of parliament. A comparable system was implemented at the faculty level, with a faculty board

59. Discussion meeting in the Academy Building on the introduction of a new democratic governance model (1968), with Rector Magnificus Jan Snijders (standing behind the table) and student representative Jacques Wallage (left at the table).

60. *Occupation of the Academy Building in protest against increased tuition fees (1972).*

and a faculty council. The departmental boards were put in charge of teaching and research policy, with the monopoly of individual professors forever relegated to the past.

Groningen did give this new governance model its own twist by granting students and staff maximal participation within the law. For example, one student and one technical staff member were invited to join the board of the university as advisors. Even with the introduction of new laws that further reduced the influence of the university council, the University of Groningen has remained faithful to its 'harmony model' to this very day.

In the 1970s, the university and faculty councils became the scene of endless debates on the university's trajectory. These debates were reported on a weekly basis in the independent university newspaper the *UK*, launched in 1971 as a watchdog of the democratic process. Various themes were discussed, from student housing and working conditions to large-scale social issues such as aid for war-torn Vietnam, condemnation of the military regime in Chile, or the boycott of the apartheid government in South Africa. Critics believed that these kinds of broad discussions undermined the university's administrative power.

The democratization of the university cannot be seen as separate from the cultural revolution of the 1960s that began in the US and spread to Europe. The

Paris Uprising of May 1968 became the symbol of this anti-authoritarian revolt, which was accompanied by demonstrations, occupations and other extra-parliamentary actions. In the Netherlands, the five-day occupation of the Maagdenhuis – the administrative heart of the University of Amsterdam – in 1969 led to much publicity and commotion. In Groningen, university buildings were also occupied, and protest actions were organized by the left-wing student union the GSb (*Groninger Studentenbond*), for example, against increased tuition fees and for more direct student influence on the curriculum. What was unique to Groningen, however, was the open-minded attitude of the administrators, who genuinely took students seriously and were even pleased that they were involved in the democratization process. This led to Groningen being known in the Netherlands as a moderate progressive university where parents could send their children to without concern.

61. *Students protesting against budget cuts at a meeting of the university council (1974).*

6 /

62. In 1987, the Aula of the Academy Building was given a new mural: 'The Tree of Knowledge', painted by the artists Wout Muller and Matthijs Röling, the son of law professor Bernard Röling.

Professionalism with a touch of idealism (1980-2000)

S tarting in the 1980s, a new wind began to blow through Dutch academia. As a result of the explosive increase in student and staff numbers and the surge of new, often small-scale degree programmes, higher education was becoming too expensive. The education minister intervened, and the universities were forced to reduce their degree offerings. The days in which students could study for ten or more years at the government's expense were a thing of the past. For the first time in its history, the University of Groningen formulated an international policy of its own aimed primarily at development cooperation. The university skilfully capitalized on important developments in world politics such as the fall of the Berlin Wall and the collapse of the Eastern Bloc. This was not driven by idealism alone: free-market principles and a more commercial approach were increasingly gaining ground.

The extinction of the eternal student

One problem that universities had been facing since the 1950s was the long-term student. In the early 1960s, the Minister of Education had tried to reduce the duration of study to five years, but in practice, students often took seven to eight years to complete a degree. The 'eternal student' who spent over a decade studying, often while engaging in various extracurricular activities, was a well-known phenomenon.

It was only in the 1980s that the tide turned. Under pressure from an economic recession triggered by the oil crisis, the ever-growing costs of education became untenable, despite a lower growth rate in student numbers. Dutch universities were almost entirely funded by the central government, and students with less wealthy parents benefited from generous grants and loans. This free access to university education was a great common good, but it also led to unmanageable costs.

63. *Students of cultural anthropology protest against the closure of their studies (in the middle professor of cultural anthropology Adriaan Prins), 1982.*

One of the most obvious ways to cut costs was to reduce the duration of study. From 1982 onwards, all degree programmes were reduced to a maximum of four years. This measure had some effect: the study pace slowly increased, and long-term students became rare. The measure became more effective when it was coupled with financial incentives. As of 1986, students who exceeded their maximum duration by more than two years were forced to pay for the rest of their study themselves. In the 1990s, the grant system was further tightened by the introduction of a performance grant: students who took too long to complete their degree had to repay part of the grant. Despite these measures, well over 50% of students still took six years to complete a four-year programme. It was only with the 2010 introduction of the Binding Study Advice that the University of Groningen – as one of the last in the Netherlands – seriously tackled this persistent problem. Students were now required to complete at least two-thirds of their first-year credit points in their first year of study. Those who did not were not allowed to proceed with the degree programme.

Dutch universities are quite similar to each other in terms of level and study offerings. Unlike the United States, there is no Dutch equivalent of the Ivy League, and most universities offer a broad range of degree programmes with minimum distinctiveness. The 1960s witnessed a proliferation of experimental degree programmes that often capitalized on the wishes of the labour market. The Dutch government stimulated this development in an attempt to accommodate growing student numbers. In the 1970s and 1980s, Groningen introduced new degree programmes in computer science, business administration, general language and culture, educational sciences and cultural anthropology.

However, government policy changed as a result of further budget cuts. Universities were told to define stronger individual identities for themselves and to focus on offering programmes in disciplines in which they excelled. The education minister believed it no longer made sense for every university to offer the same broad range of degree programmes. In Groningen, this led to the almost immediate closure of the degree programme in cultural anthropology and the cancellation of other small-scale programmes such as Egyptology and Indo-Iranian studies. Even philosophy came under pressure and could only be kept after much effort was put into pleading its case. The most painful closure was dentistry, which had recently acquired a new building and been made into an autonomous faculty. The minister had concluded that five degree programmes in dentistry was too much for the Netherlands, especially since the labour market was flooded with recently graduated dentists. Two programmes had to close down, and the choice fell on either Groningen or Utrecht. Both universities vehe-

64. Blockade of the dentistry building in protest against the closure of the Groningen Faculty of Dentistry (1987).

mently resisted the closure, arguing that according to their prognoses, a shortage of dentists was imminent. The minister and the House of Representatives were unimpressed. In 1991, the Groningen Faculty of Dentistry was forced to close its doors ... only to re-open a mere four years later. The predicted shortage of dentists had materialized, and there was urgent need for an additional dentistry department. The board of the university denounced this clear example of governmental mismanagement but made a virtue of necessity. The new degree programme entered into a unique form of collaboration with the dental hygiene programme of the Hanze University of Applied Sciences and quickly became a leader within the Netherlands.

In the long run, the division of labour among Dutch universities had a limited effect, with the number of new degree programmes growing progressively. With programmes such as journalism and industrial engineering and management, the University of Groningen responded to the wishes of the labour market. The intended sharp profiling and competition among universities, vaguely inspired by the American system, never really took off. In the hunt for popular degree programmes that would deliver more students and funding, university offerings became possibly even more homogenous than before. What did happen was that budget constraints led Dutch universities to develop a more corporate model.

Long-term relationship with Ouagadougou

From the late 1960s onwards, the University of Groningen increasingly prioritized its social role with the hope of making a serious contribution to the development of what was then referred to as Third World countries. In 1976, the university council decided that 5% of the university's research should henceforth be 'relevant to development aid'. Public lectures, symposiums, training weeks and simulation games were organized to bring the chasm between the global north and south to the students' attention. Questions of war and peace were also discussed, with frequent appearances by the Groningen professor of conflict studies, Bernard Röling.

In 1969, a small-scale *Bureau Buitenland* (International Bureau) was established to manage these activities, which was not always an easy task. For example, Groningen was keen to establish contacts with universities in the Soviet Union to break through 'mutual fixed prejudices'. Members of Russian youth organizations were invited to visit Groningen in December 1971, and after an extended preparation period, a select group of 27 Groningen students was allowed to visit the universities of Leningrad, Moscow and Erevan (the capital of Armenia) in 1974. There was, however, no follow-up. An ongoing exchange relationship with

65. *The military war tribunal in Tokyo with Bernard Röling (back row, second from left).*

Bernard Röling

ernard Röling (1906-1985) was an idiosyncratic jurist who studied criminal law, international law and the science of war and peace. He gained international fame as a judge at the military war tribunal in Tokyo for the prosecution of Japanese war criminals (1946-1948), where he was the only one among ten judges to take a dissenting stance. Despite pressure from the Dutch government, he maintained his well-documented position that some of the accused should be acquitted. As a member of the Dutch delegation to the General Assembly of the United Nations, he also took controversial positions on post-colonial issues. In 1949, Röling was appointed professor of criminal law in Groningen, but his interest increasingly shifted to the international law of war. In 1962, he established the Polemological Institute to study matters concerning war and peace. Due to his wide knowledge of court records, Röling was an international authority in the field of peace and security policy, and he laid the foundation for the degree programme in international relations. He was famous among the general public for his television lectures on war and peace, his principled rejection of nuclear weapons (which he called 'a crime against humanity') and his criticism of US involvement in the Vietnam War.

66. *Paramanga Ernest Yonli, future Prime Minister of Burkina Faso, receives a PhD in economics at the Groningen University and is congratulated by his supervisor Caspar Schweigman, director of the Centre of Development Studies (1997).*

the University of Erevan was too sensitive an issue for the Soviet authorities, who refused to grant the Armenians permission for a return visit.

The University of Groningen was more successful in establishing long-term relationships with the University of Ouagadougou in Burkina Faso and the Eduardo Mondlane University in Mozambique. Starting in the late 1970s and at the request of the Dutch organization for the internationalization of education (Nuffic), Groningen explored possibilities for collaboration with Burkina Faso (known at the time as the Republic of Upper Volta), a West African country known for its relative stability. Groningen already had some contacts at the University of Ouagadougou, where a Groningen teaching methodology expert was helping to develop the physics curriculum. This formed the starting point for further collaboration. Groningen field workers trained Burkinabe lecturers and advised the young university on its structure. Aside from physics, Groningen helped organize degree programmes in mathematics, ecology, economics and econometrics.

This resulted in a strong and lasting relationship with the African university, one that survived repeated pressures. When the revolutionary president, Thomas Sankara, was deposed in 1987 after a coup, the University of Groningen had to decide whether to stay or go. It decided to stay in the belief that the young university was in need of support more than ever. The situation became even more difficult when the university's long-time Burkinabe contact person on the collaboration project, Guillaume Sessouma, was arrested and murdered in late 1989.

Once again, the university faced the dilemma: pull out or go on? Groningen administrators were divided on the matter, as were the Burkina Faso staff. As recollected by Madeleine Gardeur, head of *Bureau Buitenland*: 'In the end, the deciding factor was an appeal from the Burkinabe university staff: "Please stay or we'll be in even greater danger!"'

In the 1990s, the political situation in Burkina Faso stabilized as a result of economic growth. Collaboration was extended to disciplines such as journalism. A number of African researchers defended their theses in Groningen, including Paramanga Ernest Yonli, who later became Prime Minister of his country. Funding was discontinued in 2005, but collaboration continued in the field of ecology and environmental studies.

Erasmus and Marco Polo

Collaboration with developing countries only represented a small portion of the international relations the university has built throughout the years. Professors

67. Former UG rector and president of the board Eric Bleumink and Abdella Mohammed Oumer, an Ethiopian student of economics who studied with the financial support of the Eric Bleumink Fund. Since 2000, the Eric Bleumink Fund has awarded more than 70 scholarships to talented students from developing countries.

68. Helmut Kohl, the former chancellor of Germany, was awarded an honorary doctorate on the occasion of the university's 385th anniversary. The postponed presentation, a year later, in 1999, was overshadowed by revelations about secret funds from Kohl's party, the Christian Democratic Union (CDU). Rector Magnificus Doeko Bosscher (right) defended the award.

and research groups had their own international partners with whom they engaged in intense collaboration or simply exchanged experiences. Taking stock in 1986, the University of Groningen was able to boast a wide network of 650 official international relationships. One in three staff members went abroad at least once a year or received international guests. These contacts primarily centred on research projects, with the faculties of medicine, mathematics and natural sciences leading the way. The most popular country among Groningen researchers was the US, followed by West Germany. Half of all contacts involved colleagues from Western Europe, one quarter from North America, and only 15% from developing countries in Africa and Asia. Although this was a rough inventory, Rector Magnificus Eric Bleumink believed it made the importance of international collaboration abundantly clear: 'Research groups and disciplines that lose contact with the international market are doomed.'

International research policy was still primarily the domain of faculties and departments. The univeristy's central policy focused on development projects and increasingly on student exchanges. Dutch students were quite attached to their home ground: only 1% could be convinced to go abroad for a degree programme or internship. The 1987 introduction of the Erasmus Programme, a funding programme established by the European Community for student exchange, and the 1996 advent of Groningen's own Marco Polo grant scheme helped increase mobility. Still, the figures remained modest: approximately 300 to 400 Groningen students a year went abroad on an Erasmus grant, and the number of incoming international students was lower still. The Dutch language was a problem for international students, and courses in English were still rare.

The University of Groningen was on many occasions successful in capitalizing on international developments. In early 1990, when the Berlin Wall fell and the Eastern Bloc collapsed, the university immediately contacted universities in Hungary and Czechoslovakia. Another opportunity for contact arose a few years later. After the Dutch government had expressed criticism of human rights violations in Indonesia, which in turn led to a lengthy conflict between the two countries, Indonesia broke off development relationships, causing a number of Dutch universities to retreat. The University of Groningen made good use of this situation. A Groningen delegation visited Indonesia and managed to regain the trust of the Indonesians. In 1999, the university launched a double-degree programme with the Institut Teknologi Bandung and the Universitas Gadjah Mada in Yogyakarta. This degree programme was unique in the Netherlands: students could study in Groningen and Bandung and received a degree certificate from both universities. This system became a great success and was later extended to other strategic partners in Indonesia, China, Hungary and Germany.

On to the market

From the 1980s onwards, the university could no longer rely on generous funding from the Dutch government, forcing the Groningen academics to take their first cautious steps into the market. In 1981, the university created a *Transferbureau* (Transfer Department) aimed at strengthening relations with small and medium-sized enterprises. This was followed three years later by the official launch of the Science Park, initiated by biochemistry professor Bernard Witholt, who had spent some time in the US. His ideal was a Groningen Silicon Valley according to the American model with a range of innovative high-tech companies closely linked to the university's research groups. The Paddepoel campus was an ideal location for this project. Witholt's plans were met with the usual reservations. Would the university not surrender to the corporate sector? Would this kind of collaboration not harm freedom of research? Witholt pushed through and gained financial support for his plan. A business centre was created where starters could experiment under guidance. One of the first large companies to join was Mediware, a

69. *Building of the Datacenter Bytes Net at the Zernike Science Park (2018).*

developer of computer equipment for precise dosing of medicines. The company worked in close collaboration with the Department of Pharmaceutical Studies. The Zernike Science Park, named after Groningen Nobel Prize laureate Frits Zernike, slowly grew. Eight years after its opening, it was home to 50 relatively profitable businesses, with a total staff of approximately 250.

The first university in the Netherlands to promote itself as an 'entrepreneurial university' was the University of Twente. Without attempting to follow their example, the board of the University of Groningen stimulated faculties to enter the market and be more enterprising. But stimulating entrepreneurship also had a shadow side to it. Professors and researchers started their own commercial foundations hidden from the administration. In the early 1990s, the university had an estimated 50 such foundations. In the medical, natural sciences and law departments, in particular, enterprising professors had created their own personal 'businesses'. This had to stop. The foundation boards were called to account for their financial policies and were instructed to adhere to university regulations. 'The era of amateurism, with people doing their bookkeeping on a Saturday morning at the breakfast table, is over', said the president of the board of the university, Eric Bleumink, in the university newspaper *UK*: 'We need a cultural shift.'

So where did the University of Groningen stand on the eve of the 21st century? In his inaugural speech as rector at the opening of the academic year 1996-1997, the physicist Folkert van der Woude took a moment to take stock. One thing was clear, he said: free-market principles had become the norm. The government saw academic research and education primarily as driving engines for the economy, 'in direct opposition to the model that shaped university life for centuries and was based on academic freedom'. The rector feared that curiosity-driven research would be supplanted by economy-driven research and strongly advocated a healthy balance. He probably knew that the trend was unstoppable, and rather than resist it, he chose to take a leap forward instead. If research and education were to be at the service of the economy, he argued, we should work towards a better future. Given that ecological factors will sooner or later force a growth economy to make room for a more sustainable model, Van der Woude suggested that universities put their academic freedom to good use and take the lead in transitioning to and investing in 'ecology-driven' research. This was a visionary call to action that was somewhat ahead of its time.

From the late 1990s onwards, the Dutch government increasingly pushed universities to become social enterprises based on key concepts such as efficiency and excellence. Good business management required adjustments within the administration. In 1997, the new Modernization of University Governance Act (MUB) was passed, reducing the power of the university and faculty councils. University administration became more hierarchical and commercial. The University of Groningen tried to remain faithful to its own harmony model, which was based on consensus between various administrative bodies, but the days that students could participate in charting the course of research and expansion policy were over. The commercial university was well on its way to becoming the norm.

7 /

70. *Professor Ben Feringa and his international research team celebrate winning the 2016 Nobel Prize in Chemistry.*

The global university (2000-today)

For a long time, the University of Groningen had strong roots in its own region and modest international ambitions. This began to change in the first decade of the 21st century. After years of moderate growth, international student and staff numbers suddenly grew by leaps and bounds. At the same time, the university began to rise in international rankings. The brain behind this policy was the ambitious president of the board of the university, Sibrand Poppema, who dreamt of putting Groningen on the map as an international research university. But his ambition went even further than that: his goal was for Groningen to become internationally renowned with a campus in China. A plan that met with much resistance.

The world as a stage

In early 2020, a casual passer-by strolling across the Academieplein or Zernike Campus is more likely to be accosted in English than in Dutch. With almost 8,000 international Bachelor's and Master's students from 125 different countries (out of a total of 33,000 students), the University of Groningen is a serious player in the international student market. In comparison, Groningen only had 300 regular international students at the turn of the century, mostly from Germany, followed at some distance by China. An incredible metamorphosis had taken place in less than 20 years.

In the late 1990s, attention shifted from recruiting and sending students abroad to actively attracting regular students. The university campaigned in Germany and attended international education fairs in Asia and Latin America. More attention was devoted to welcoming and guiding international students who, starting in 2002, were met with a welcoming ceremony first held in the Aula of the Academy Building, and when that became too small in the Martinikerk and cultural centre De Oosterpoort. The international staff numbers were also growing fast. Whereas in 2006 less than one-quarter of the research staff (including

71. Welcoming ceremony for international students in the Martinikerk. In the first row, Sibrand Poppema, president of the board of the university.

PhD students) came from abroad, by 2018 this figure had increased to nearly 50%. How did the university manage to dramatically increase international student and staff numbers in such a short period of time?

The first step was the introduction of a uniform Bachelor's and Master's system to replace a Dutch educational system that was often incomprehensible to outsiders. In 1999, the Ministers of Education from 29 European countries met in Bologna to sign an agreement on a uniform system of higher education for all European countries. This made it possible for students to study abroad without formal limitations. The Bologna Process led to the introduction of Bachelor's and Master's titles based on the Anglo-Saxon model. The Dutch Minister of Education put pressure on the universities, and as early as 2002, the first Groningen faculties were implementing what became known as the BaMa system.

Another condition for successfully recruiting international students was the development of new English-language degree programmes. This process got off to a slower-than-expected start during the difficult years of transition to the BaMa system. In 2006, a committee led by Rector Magnificus Frans Zwarts launched an ambitious plan, outlined in a document entitled *The World as a Stage*, by which Groningen would quickly grow into an international university where 'the best students from all over the world would want to study'. Strikingly, the Zwarts Committee listed hard target figures: by 2014, on the occasion of its 400th anniversary, the University of Groningen should have enough capacity to accommodate more than 5,000 international students (a fivefold increase); all Master's programmes and 20% of Bachelor's programmes should be taught in English (a twofold increase); and international staff should have doubled. All of this was to be accomplished in eight years. This seemed very ambitious at the time and many doubted the plan's feasibility, but having such a plan did speed things up, aided in part by the arrival of Sibrand Poppema, the ambitious president of the board of the university who dreamed of making the University of Groningen a serious world player. The number of international students and staff skyrocketed, and by the time of the 400th anniversary celebration, nearly all of Zwarts' objectives had been partially or fully met. A few years later, more than half of all Bachelor's programmes and nearly all Master's and PhD programmes were taught in English.

The Anglicization of the university was not to everyone's taste. Douwe Draaisma, a professor of psychology, warned in 2005 in his inaugural lecture entitled *Het verdriet van de kosmopoliet* (The Sorrow of the Cosmopolitan) against a one-sided fixation on Anglo-Saxon scientific literature and English as a language of instruction. In his opinion, internationalization should broaden the university's horizon to include diverse cultures and preserve important academic languages such as German and French. With a growing number of English-language degree programmes, some feared that Dutch would no longer exist as an

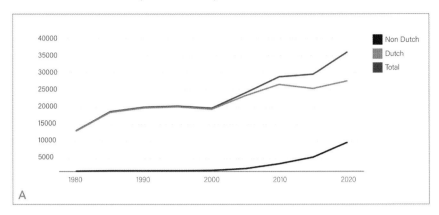

A

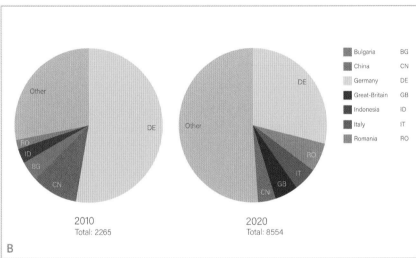

B

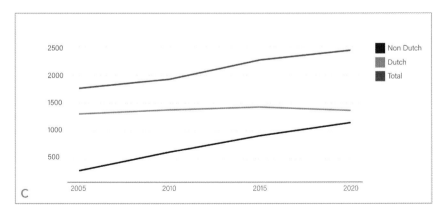

C

72. Graphs: A. Non-Dutch students UG; B. Nationalities of foreign students (top 5); C. Academic staff UG in FTE.

73. *Rector Magnificus Frans Zwarts (left) addresses the Indonesian Minister of Education.*

academic language. There were also complaints from student unions about lecturers' insufficient command of English and the effect this had on the quality of teaching. The university responded by instituting compulsory English language courses for all lecturers. Another issue was international student housing. This turned out to be a persistent problem, with emergency buildings and even tent camps having to be set up to provide newcomers with temporary accommodation at the start of each academic year.

As far as teaching was concerned, the mass arrival of international students led to the introduction of new educational methods. Rector Magnificus Elmer Sterken, who took over from Frans Zwarts in 2011, emerged as a committed advocate of the active learning environment, an approach that capitalized on the cultural background of students from different countries. Sterken embraced the American concept of learning communities: students and lecturers actively working together to solve problems and draw on each other's expertise. This offered opportunities for a university with an international student population to devote explicit attention to students' cultural backgrounds.

From 2013 onwards, a number of faculties experimented with this new approach, initially with varying degrees of success. English proficiency among students and lecturers, in particular, left much to be desired at times, and fruitful cultural interaction only worked within well-balanced groups.

International research university

In the field of research, the University of Groningen also worked to further improve its international reputation. Starting in the late 1990s, Groningen distinguished itself through its top research schools such as the Materials Science Centre (Zernike Institute for Advanced Materials) and the Netherlands Research School for Astronomy (NOVA) in which Groningen astronomers played an important role. Striving for excellence was no longer anathema in the traditionally egalitarian Netherlands, and Groningen presented itself as a place where talent was given every opportunity to flourish. Talented students were offered in-depth honours programmes and an interdisciplinary University College. Excellent young researchers were ushered through a sophisticated career track based on the American model (tenure track), leading to an appointment as professor within ten years.

74. January 2007, Sibrand Poppema, dean of the Faculty of Medicine, welcomes the first scholarship students from Saudi Arabia in Groningen. Annually, 25 to 30 students start in a foundation year that prepares for the English-track Bachelor's programme in medicine. About 70% succeed and start with the bachelor programme. On the side they study Dutch, which is an important requirement for being admitted to the clinical training in the Master's programme.

75. *Gymnast Epke Zonderland, student of medicine at the UG, won the gold medal on the high bar at the 2012 London Olympics. Rector Magnificus Elmer Sterken honoured him in the Aula of the Academy Building. The 'Flying Dutchman' has also captured three World Championship titles. He qualified as a medical doctor in 2018.*

The driving force behind this policy was the pathologist Sibrand Poppema who served as president of the board of the university from 2008 to 2018. During these years, Groningen became known as a research university on its way to the international top. Poppema devoted all his energy to this project. *Passion & Performance* was the title of his strategic plan for positioning the university in the international market. Poppema's ambition to push Groningen into the top 100 in the three most important international rankings of universities was realized in 2013. Although this kind of benchmarking was subject to a certain degree of

76. In 1997, the academic hospital opened a new medical building with a central reception hall and covered streets connecting the various clinics. Eight years later, the Faculty of Medicine of the University of Groningen and the Academic Hospital Groningen merged into a new organization: the University Medical Center Groningen (UMCG).

scorn, and even though differences with other Dutch classical universities remained minimal, Groningen's newly acquired position nevertheless gave it more international recruiting power.

Top-notch research requires international and interdisciplinary collaboration. A good example of this was LOFAR, a giant radio telescope with a network of thousands of sensors spread over an area with a diameter of 100 kilometres in the northern Netherlands and Germany. This network was linked to an IB Blue Gene supercomputer at the university computing centre, turning Groningen into a top player in the field of big data. Since 2010, LOFAR has brought together computer scientists, astronomers, geophysicists and agricultural researchers. The network is linked to antennas in Germany, Great Britain, France, Sweden and Poland.

In the race for European research funds, a clear profile of socially relevant research became ever more important. In 2011, Groningen presented its three areas of focus: energy, healthy ageing and a sustainable society. These research themes involved various disciplines and partners. Healthy ageing, for example, involved nearly all faculties and stimulated collaboration with the University Medical Center Groningen and the Hanze University of Applied Sciences in the Aletta Jacobs School of Public Health.

The trend towards more funding and attention to socially as well as economically relevant research led to dissenting voices from critics warning against the neglect of 'curiosity-driven' fundamental research. One of them was Ben Feringa, an organic chemistry professor who won a Nobel Prize in 2016 for developing molecular machines. A 'molecular engineer', Feringa worked tirelessly for decades with a team of young researchers from different countries to develop molecular nano-systems: a clear example of free research not directly driven by any potential applications. This was only the second Nobel Prize for the University of Groningen, and it was celebrated in style with an academic ceremony in a packed Martinikerk. What a difference this was from 1953 when physics professor Frits Zernike won the Nobel Prize for his phase contrast microscope and treated his colleagues to rum bonbons before promptly returning to work.

In addition to the Nobel Prize, there is the Dutch equivalent for groundbreaking research called the Spinoza Prize. Between 1995 and 2014, only three researchers from the University of Groningen won this prize: George Sawatzky (materials science), Dirkje Postma (pathophysiology of breathing) and Ben Feringa. But starting from 2014, the university made up for lost time, with prizes being received by Theunis Piersma (migrating bird ecology), soon-to-be Rector Magnificus Cisca Wijmenga (human genetics), Bart van Wees (technical physics), Lodi Nauta (history of philosophy), Amina Helmi (formation of the Milky Way) and Pauline Kleingeld (ethics). This clearly shows that top research covered a much wider range than the university's three social research themes, with a leading role for female researchers in recent years.

77. The Argentinian born astronomer Amina Helmi won the prestigious Spinoza Price 2019.

78. Nobel prize laureate Ben Feringa shows a life-size representation of his nanocar at the Grote Markt square in the centre of Groningen.

Second Nobel Prize – the nanocar

Ben Feringa (1951) is an enthusiastic science ambassador. With his inspiring appearances in lecture halls and television programmes, he knows how to captivate public interest in his narrative of fundamental research as a voyage of discovery with unpredictable outcomes. Feringa studied chemistry and defended his PhD in Groningen, worked for a while at Shell and returned to his alma mater in 1984, where he followed in the steps of his PhD supervisor and teacher Hans Wijnberg and was appointed professor of organic chemistry in 1988. In the 1990s, Feringa and his research team discovered that molecular bonds could make a propeller turn under the influence of light flashes. This allowed them to develop a simple nano-sized molecular motor. Upon receiving the 2014 Spinoza Prize for his ground-breaking work, Feringa announced his intention to use the prize money to build a molecular car. Seven years later, his light-powered nanocar, a molecular four-wheel drive, appeared on the cover of the science journal *Nature*. Feringa was awarded many international prizes for his ground-breaking research, including a Nobel Prize in Chemistry in 2016, shared with his international colleagues Jean-Pierre Sauvage and James Fraser Stoddart, for developing molecular nanomachines. Feringa insisted that this was a team effort, and at the award ceremony in the Martinikerk he called his entire research group onto the stage to share the honour.

Campus Yantai and Campus Fryslân

At the honorary doctorate presentation on the occasion of the university's 400th anniversary, Rector Magnificus Elmer Sterken ventured to predict the future. He forecasts that in the year 2064 the University of Groningen would still retain its traditionally strong link to the region but also be a serious world player: 'Student mobility will go back to 17th-century Dutch levels, with the University of Groningen being part of an international network with various campuses all over the world.' The first such campus was planned in the Chinese city of Yantai. However, the idea of creating Groningen campuses on various continents, inspired by President Poppema, turned out to be more difficult than expected.

For years, the university had worked towards building a strong relationship with China, and a growing number of Chinese students and PhD students were finding their way to Groningen. Particularly strong ties were forged with Fudan, a top university in Shanghai. In 2007, the University of Groningen established a Dutch Studies Centre in Shanghai, teaching Dutch and European culture, economics and politics, and other subjects. With the foundation of the Confucius Institute, China also claimed a cultural base in Groningen. Collaboration with Communist China met with little resistance at first. This changed in 2015 when President Poppema launched an ambitious plan for Groningen to become the first Dutch university to establish an international branch campus at the China Agricultural University in the Yantai metropolis. Approximately 10,000 Chinese students would complete a full-fledged University of Groningen degree programme, obtain a Groningen degree certificate, and spend time studying in Groningen.

The Chinese adventure initially seemed very promising. In October 2015, an initial agreement was signed in the presence of the Dutch King Willem Alexander and President Xi Jinping of the People's Republic of China. But the plans quickly led to discord, both within the university and in Dutch politics at large. Doubts were expressed concerning its financial feasibility and the safeguarding of academic freedom in China. The Faculty of Economics and Business – which was supposed to be the first to start in Yantai, along with the Faculty of Science and Engineering (formerly the Faculty of Mathematics and Natural Sciences) – pulled out, saying it had as yet insufficient faith in the business plan. It was replaced by the Faculty of Spatial Sciences. Poppema defended his plan with verve. Decreasing birth rates in the Netherlands meant a lower influx of Dutch students after 2022, and the Chinese campus would allow Groningen to continue to grow into a major global university. Furthermore, a more intensive relationship with China, home to so much top talent, would benefit the quality of Groningen teaching and research. Poppema argued that this was 'a unique opportunity', an opinion

79. The University of Groningen signed an agreement with the Chinese Agricultural University and the city of Yantai on the funding of a branch campus in China. Dutch King Willem-Alexander and Chinese President Xi Jinping were among the attendees (2015).

shared by the more than 100 professors who supported him in an open letter to the newspapers.

After some resistance, the House of Representatives agreed to a legal amendment to make the plan possible, but the Minister of Education set an additional condition by requiring the university council to give its consent. And this was where things went astray. A large majority within the council found the adventure too risky, despite attempts by the university board to accommodate the reservations. The much-praised harmony model failed to work this time, and in 2018 the board was forced to recall its plan for transnational education in Yantai. Was this a missed opportunity or a wise decision? On this, too, opinions remain divided.

However, satellite expansion did materialize within the Netherlands. Coinciding with the Yantai adventure, the University of Groningen launched a plan for a campus in Leeuwarden, the capital of the neighbouring province of Friesland. Municipal and provincial government authorities wished to strengthen the academic climate in Leeuwarden, and a plan was crafted for a faculty offering a broad interdisciplinary Bachelor's degree programme and ten Master's degree programmes: Campus Fryslân. With regional and international themes such as global responsibility and leadership, multilingualism, and health and food, the faculty targeted Frisian and other Dutch students as well as students from abroad. In 2018, the first cohort started their Bachelor's programme, and by 2025 Cam-

80. *Linnaeusborg, Center for Life Sciences. Architect: Rudy Uytenhaak (2011).*

pus Fryslân is expected to be home to approximately 1,000 students and 50 PhD students. Academic education and research are once again back in Friesland after a long absence since the 1811 closure of the University of Franeker (apart from a short period around 1980 during which a part of the Groningen Faculty of Social Sciences was located in Leeuwarden).

A multicultural community

More than four centuries after its foundation, the University of Groningen continues to be solidly anchored in the city and the region. More than ever, Groningen is a real student city, with more than 60,000 students of the University of Groningen and the Hanze University of Applied Sciences out of a total population of 230,000. In 400 years, the university has grown to include 11 faculties, with the University College and Campus Fryslân as its newest additions. The Faculties of Economics and Business Administration fused in 2007, and in 2005 the Faculty of Medical Sciences merged with the University Medical Center Groningen (UMCG), integrating academic teaching and research with specialist training and patient care at the Academic Hospital.

The university is spread out across the city, remaining faithful to the contours of the three-centre plan of 1958. The administrative heart of the university is still located in the city centre. The triangle of the Academy Building, the University Library and the Harmonie Building – home to the Faculties of Arts and Law – has grown into a lively city campus with cafés and restaurants and endless rows of bicycles dominating the street view. At walking distance from this cluster, we find the Faculties of Theology and Religious Studies, Philosophy, and Behavioural and Social Sciences. The second centre consists of the UMCG grounds, the Healthy Ageing Campus, with centrepieces such as the 2013 ERIBA building (European Research Institute for Biology of Ageing) and the Proton Centre, the first of its kind in the Netherlands, where a select group of young cancer patients have received treatment since 2018. The third centre, the Zernike Complex at Paddepoel, forms the university's external campus. It is home to the faculties of Economics and Business, Spatial Sciences, and Science and Engineering, and includes the biology department, which moved to the village of Haren in the 1960s only to return in 2010 to the new and beautifully designed Linnaeusborg. In 2016, University of Groningen researchers on energy came together in the most sustainable building of the Netherlands, the Energy Academy. The university and its three centres overlay the city as a kind of archipelago.

In addition to being embedded within the region, the University of Groningen has also emerged as a serious 21st-century world player. It is a prominent mem-

81. Energy Academy Europe. Architects: Broekbakema and De Unie Architecten (2017).   127

82. Conference of the Coimbra Group, an association of 41 long-established European universities, in Groningen, as part of the university's 400th anniversary celebration (2014).

---

ber of the Coimbra Group, a network of 39 long-established European universities, and maintains close strategic ties with the universities of Ghent (Belgium), Göttingen (Germany), Uppsala (Sweden) and more recently Tartu (Estonia) in the U4Society Network. With nearly 10,000 international students and staff, Groningen can safely claim its position as an internationally oriented university, with nothing to fear from controllers in The Hague. The university therefore quite deliberately chose the theme *For Infinity* (4∞) for its 400th anniversary celebration. A modern variation on the 1614 Eternal Edict, it showed that the university's old fear of closure or curtailment had made way for irrepressible optimism.

Five years later, the university used the lustrum theme *All Inclusive* to express its wish to form an open and diverse community in which all 6,000 staff members and 32,000 students felt at home. This turned out to be quite a challenge. In less than 20 years, the university had grown into a multicultural institution with students and researchers from 125 different countries, which sometimes caused

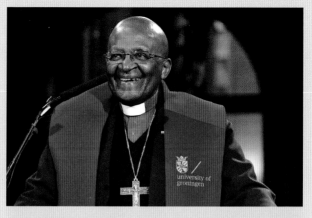

83. In September 2012, the UG awarded an honorary doctorate in theology and religious studies to the South African Archbishop Desmond Tutu.

underlying tensions. A survey by the university newspaper, the *UKrant*, revealed that international students were frequently the victim of cultural prejudices and stereotyping – an experience hardly in line with the university's language and culture policy and its embraced principle of the *international classroom* centred on appreciating and learning from cultural differences. Jokes about other people's cultures are less innocent than they might seem, said Rector Magnificus Sterken in response to the survey. The time had come for an awareness-raising campaign.

A bigger hurdle to creating an inclusive and diverse academic community was the imbalanced gender ratio, a persistent problem facing all Dutch universities. While female students have been in the majority for years, less than 25% of professors and only 40% of the staff were women. With the Rosalind Franklin programme launched in 2002, the University of Groningen offered women a fast track to professorship, but this has not been enough to achieve the balance. A truly diverse university was clearly a long-term project. However, an important

step forward was taken in 2019 with the appointment of the first female rector, the Spinoza Prize laureate Cisca Wijmenga.

The Coronavirus pandemic

With the inauguration of a completely new board in 2018-2019, the University of Groningen entered a new chapter in its history. The still smouldering plan for a campus in China was finally put to rest, and the university's anchoring in its own region was reinforced with the launch of the University of the North, a collaborative project between the University of Groningen and universities of applied sciences in the North of the Netherlands centred on energy transition, public health and digitalization. These ambitious plans were temporarily shifted to the background in the spring of 2020 when the Netherlands was taken by surprise with the rapid advance of the SARS-CoV-2 virus. There followed a month-long lockdown, and academic institutions were forced for the first time in their

85. *A sober opening of the Academic Year 2020-2021 in September 2020, due to the corona virus pandemic. The guest speaker was Sigrid Kaag, Minister of Foreign Trade.*

history to close their doors to students and a large majority of research staff. The coronavirus pandemic turned working from home and remote learning into the new norm. Some feared that this would greatly reduce the influx of international students. Faculties anticipated that the academic year 2020-2021 would be marked by a severe decrease in the number of new students due to travelling restrictions and the prospect of mostly remote learning and social distancing. This turned out to be too pessimistic. Although exchange programmes for guest students coming to the Netherlands for a limited period did come to a near standstill, this did not apply to regular international students. At the start of the academic year, the University of Groningen was able to boast a total of 8,554 international students, a record figure and an increase of 800 compared to the previous year. Most of these new international recruits came from other European countries. The total number of students also increased by nearly 10% to reach 36,000, another record. As a result of the coronavirus pandemic, a greater number of early school leavers in the Netherlands obtained a degree certificate and, instead of taking a gap year, immediately enrolled in a university degree programme.

Universities have worked hard to keep teaching and to continue research as much as possible with the help of online lectures, remote examinations and on-line work meetings. Without a doubt, this crisis and the risk of new epidemics will greatly affect the way that universities will be organized in the future. Only time will tell how this pandemic will ultimately affect teaching and research at the University of Groningen.

Acknowledgements

Illustrations

ANP, Koen van Weel: fig. 79
Archief Vindicat: fig. 37
Piet Boonstra: fig. 59
Reyer Boxem: fig. 29
Collection Amsterdam Museum: fig. 15
Collection Rijksmuseum Amsterdam: fig. 12, 21
Collection UKrant: fig. 60-61
Collection University Museum Groningen: fig. 4-9, 11, 13-14, 16-20, 22-28, 30-36, 38-39, 41-43, 45-53, 55-58, 62, 65, 76
P. Cramer, RHC Groninger Archieven: fig. 40
Kloostermuseum Aduard: fig. 2
Michel de Groot: fig. 68, 73-74
Daniël Houben: fig. 72
Jeroen van Kooten: page 8
RHC Groninger Archieven: fig. 1
Elmer Spaargaren: fig. 54, 63-64, 66-67, 69, 75 (below)
University library Amsterdam: fig. 6
University of Groningen (UG): fig. 3, 46, 70, 75 (above), 78, 82-83
UG, Marcel Spanjer: fig. 71, 80-81, 85
UG, Merel Weijer: fig. 77, 84
University of Groningen, Groningen Institute of Archaeology: fig. 44
Wereldaanboeken.ub.rug.nl: fig. 10

Many thanks to Renate Huttinga for her help in collecting the illustrations.

We also want to thank Christien Boomsma, Gert Gritter, Jodien Houwers, and Renzo Tuinsma for their critical comments and in particular Jouke the Vries, President of the University of Groningen, for his support and trust in producing this book.

Index

About the authors

Klaas van Berkel is Rudolf Agricola Professor of History at the University of Groningen. He is the author of *Academische Illusies* (2005), a study of the University of Groningen in times of crisis, occupation and recovery, 1930-1950 and a three-volume history of the University of Groningen, *Universiteit van het Noorden, 1614-2021* (2014-2021).

© Harry Cock

© Karel Zwaneveld

Guus Termeer was chief editor of the university weekly *UK* and head program maker of Studium Generale Groningen. He is the editor of the *Magazine 395. Grepen uit een rijke geschiedenis* (2009) and the *For Infinity 400 Magazine* (2014) about the history of the University of Groningen.